Understanding

Edited by Jock Baird.

MIDI

MUSICIAN
A Billboard Publication

Understanding Midi was originally published by **Musician Magazine**
which is a registered Trademark of Billboard Publications Inc.

Amsco Publications
London/New York/Sydney/Cologne

Exclusive Distributors:
Music Sales Limited
78 Newman Street, London W1P 3LA, England.
Music Sales Corporation
24 East 22nd Street, New York, N.Y. 10010. USA.
Music Sales Pty. Limited
27 Clarendon Street, Artarmon, Sydney, NSW 2064, Australia.

This book © Copyright 1986 by
Wise Publications.
UK ISBN 0.7119.0954.7
UK Order No. AM 63462

Cover design by Pearce Marchbank.

Music Sales complete catalogue lists thousands of titles
and is free from your local music bookshop, or direct
from Music Sales Limited.
Please send 30p in stamps for postage to:
Music Sales Limited, 78 Newman Street, London W1P 3LA.

Printed by
The Anchor Press, Tiptree, Essex.

Welcome to the Age of MIDI.

If you've been reading Musician for the nearly ten years we've been covering music, you know we're not big on equipment specials and buyer's guides—in fact, this is our first. But these are not ordinary times, and over the past year, we've become more and more convinced that the establishment and refinement of the Music Instrument Digital Interface specification in 1985 is an epochal musical event, on a par with the inventions of Bartolomeo Cristofori's 1709 pianoforte, Leo Fender's 1948 Broadcaster guitar or Bob Moog's 1964 keyboard synthesizer.

Unfortunately, the rising techno-tide has not lifted all boats. The more we talked with musicians (especially non-keyboardists), the more of the MIDI information gap we discovered. If you are one of the confused, if you see MIDI as more buzzword than real business, then this special edition is for you. In fact, in a little while, it will be required reading, because MIDI technology, coupled with the exponential spread of inexpensive quality sampling, is completely changing the way we perform and record music.

This issue begins at the beginning, the microprocessor revolution, and increases in degree of difficulty, so if you're confused, read the article before it. If what we're telling you seems obvious, skip to the next story. In looking through the Buyer's Guide, try to remember that we may have missed some lesser-known or very new pieces of equipment, especially in the software department. We were amazed to discover how much MIDI gear is available at the beginning of 1986—by the end of this year there'll be even more. When in doubt, give the manufacturer a call.

Just remember, through all the epiphanies and despair of absorbing this incredible new computer technology, that music's supposed to be fun and that MIDI's here to make it more fun. On that promise, it's already delivered. Catch the rising tide and don't miss the boat.

Coel Baird

Editor

Banish Unsightly Computer Fear!

An Introductory Pep Talk For Technophobes.
By Freff.

For some of you, the real serious technophobes, computers are no laughing matter. You've seen *2001*. You've watched *Twilight Zone* and *Voyage to the Bottom of the Sea* reruns. You know the truth: computers are soulless, dehumanizing chunks of malevolent technology bent on world conquest (and blessed with a theatrical penchant for spewing great flaming gouts of special effects sparks immediately before commercial breaks).

Above all, they have nothing to do with music. Too impersonal, man.

Well, don't try and tell the rest of us. It's too late. We're all busy having fun, which is what computers are really all about, as anybody who stops thinking Hollywood and starts thinking Honeywell finds out in short order.

This Zilog Z-80 chip helped usher in the MIDI age.

Ready for the big step? Ready to banish your unsightly computer fear... forever? All you have to do is learn the magic phrase, the sacred sacrament that sums up everything there is to know about computers.

Two words.

They're idiots.

The Computer as Absolute Moron.

Take one computer. Take one brick. Compare them. Which is smarter?

Neither of them, actually. Singly or together they haven't got the brainpower of a dead bat; if you were in the market for a paperweight the brick would be the better buy. But because human beings (those marvelous folks that brought you Trivial Pursuit, polio vaccine and *Dynasty*) were not content with paperweights that didn't do tricks, the computer was taught a few that could be shown off to the neighbors. Not quite sit, roll over and beg, but they'll do. Computers can:

1. Understand the difference between a 0 and a 1.

2. Add one number to another.

3. Subtract one number from another.

4. Compare two numbers to see which is larger.

Wow. Hot stuff. Awe-inspiring. If that's all you could do, you'd be locked away in one of those places where you aren't allowed anything sharper than a crayon.

But the thing is, they do these four tricks *very* fast. In the time it took you to read that list a decent computer could have done all those things a couple of million times. And since they don't think (forget those bad SF films; remember the dead bat) but instead just endlessly add, subtract and compare, it becomes possible for human beings to make codewords out of the 0s and 1s, assign them real meanings (like "turn on preset 37"), and then write programs that make the little buggers work to pay the rent.

Microprocessor Magic.

But, you say, I'm not ready to use a computer. Well, have you ever played a Prophet 5, or a Memorymoog, or a PolySix? Used a Drumulator or a DMX? Set your ten-dollar digital wristwatch to time a track in the studio? Do you find yourself sneering at a synth that *doesn't* have sequencers, arpeggiators and program chains? Congratulations, friend. You've already joined the computer revolution...though odds are you don't know very much about the device that made it possible.

In this case, however, ignorance is something less than bliss. Tooling around the presets on these instruments is like using a 747 to bop by the corner grocery—a gross waste of potential. And with Musical Instrumental Digital Interfaces springing up on every synth in sight, that's truer than ever. MIDI is more than just a way to let your keyboard/drum machines/whatever interface with other keyboards/drum machines/whatevers. It's nothing less than a direct line to the microprocessor itself. That means control. That means *freedom*. Learn the way that the microprocessor "thinks"—which isn't so tough, because music and programming have a lot more in common than you'd guess—and you can make it do what *you* want it to.

A microprocessor is nothing more than a small computer. So small, in fact, that the average one could fit on a fingernail with plenty of room to spare. But don't let size confuse you. The microprocessor may be tiny, but it has many things in common with its larger cousins. For one thing, it too is an idiot.

A microprocessor by itself is useless. You have to have a program to run on it. That machine language of zeroes and ones I mentioned earlier—people don't speak that very well. And it takes a *lot* of it to tell a microprocessor what to do. So in order to make it possible to write programs in less than six or seven hundred years, you use another computer—called the development system—as a translator. It takes a command in what is called *assembly language* (which still isn't English, but is at least understandable if you take the time to learn its codes) and automatically converts it into machine language, in a process called "compiling." Then, having used the development system to compile your program, you put it into a ROM, plug that into the microprocessor, and run it.

Sometimes it works and sometimes it doesn't. Microprocessors are unforgiving as well as stupid, and even the slightest mistake in a program can cause the whole thing to shut down and blurt the equivalent of a computer raspberry in your face. Which sends you back to the drawing board.

But the biggest problems don't come from the machines or the programs. They come from the human beings behind them. Designers and programmers make choices, and sometimes those choices are shortsighted, or clumsy, or limiting, or just plain wrong. Dave Rossum of E-mu Systems puts it quite bluntly: "The problems are usually just that the designers are too dumb."

Take keyboard scanning, for example. In your average synth today a microprocessor is doing many thousands of things every second, and one of those things is taking a quick scan across every key to see whether or not any of them are being pressed down. But it isn't the microprocessor that decides how fast it will scan the keys; that decision was made long before, when the instrument was first created, by a designer who might very well have opted for a slower scan time in order to free up microprocessor time to support other features. It's a tradeoff. But a slower scan time means a less responsive keyboard, and if the designer has made a mistake and chosen a scan time that's too slow, the keyboard will seem "stiff" and uncomfortable to a player. But it *isn't* the machine's fault, it's the designer's, for misusing the available resources.

So Why All the Grief?

People, of course. Those wonderful folks that brought you jargon, technophobic paranoia and programming bugs.

Computer people talk funny and use words you don't recognize. Over the years a complicated jargon has developed that covers all the thousands of little variations to be found in what are actually a pretty basic set of ideas. (You do it, too, in your own way; musicians have their own jargon.) If somebody says something you don't understand, ask them point-blank to explain it. And then be patient with their explanation, because they tend to say things like "reinitialize the operating system defaults" when they actually mean "turn the computer on."

Always remember that today's incomprehensible jargon is tomorrow's commonplace. A decade ago it was VCO and VCF. Today it's RAM and ROM. Only the acronyms change, to confuse the innocent.

Of course, it doesn't help that everything important in a computer happens "under the hood," with no moving parts to stare at. When something goes wrong it can make you feel completely helpless. The thing to remember is that

it's just a stupid machine. It isn't out to get you. It's just broken. You or a repairman can find the fault and fix it, so stay cool. A broken computer won't respond to anger any more than a dead car will repair itself if you kick its tires.

The worst, though, are bugs. Mistakes in the program. Those will drive you up the wall if you don't understand where they come from.

Remember: Computers are morons. If a program doesn't tell them exactly what to do at all times, they screw up. When you consider that really powerful programs consist of hundreds of pages of computer code...and that a single error of logic, or even just a typo, can bring the whole house of cards tumbling down...well, the miracle is that computers work at all!

It's a basic fact of Life In This Computer Age that all programs have bugs in them *somewhere*. No musician ever plays a perfect set; no programmer ever codes a perfect program. The best you can hope for in both cases is that the mistakes are so obscure nobody will ever notice them.

Self-Defense.

With computers the best defense isn't a good offense. It's a combination of knowledge, zen calm, and not taking stupid risks.

Such as...

...Computers are chock full of microchips, all sensitive to voltage surges. Power lines in America have lots of surges and spikes. So buy yourself a surge filter and put it between your computer and the wall outlet. They aren't expensive, and the safety is worth it.

...Floppy disks are just flat, round versions of magnetic recording tape. You wouldn't risk your album master near anything that could screw it up, like a radiator, direct sunlight, the studio monitors, a TV set, or your guitarist's beer; treat your floppies with the same respect.

...KEEP BACKUP COPIES. Floppy disks can wear out, just like tape. Come that day your program won't run right or your files won't load. With backups you're protected. Without them, you're out of luck.

...Get to know people who have gone through all this stuff ahead of you. Don't be afraid to ask them questions. They had to ask them once upon a time, too, so most will be glad to help you out.

...If at first you don't succeed, try again. Clichéd but true. The commonest bugs in computer programs aren't things that make a program fail outright, but instead make it fail *sometimes*. What you've got to figure out is what makes the times a program works different from the times it doesn't. Do that and you're ninety percent of the way to a fix.

...And above all, remember: *they're idiots*. Bricks. Dead bats. You're smarter than they are, and as long as you don't get angry or impatient you'll win in the end. If you feel yourself starting to lose control, go away for a while. Jog. Play air guitar. Relax. Remember how it was to learn your first instrument. Anger never forced a chord into your hand, and impatience never taught you a part. Things that are worth learning are worth respect.

Got all that? Feel more secure? Then say goodbye to fear, and hello to pleasure. The present is calling you.

I was a Computer Idiot!

Kicking and Screaming, a Guitarist Enters the Digital Age.
By Josef Woodard.

Please allow me to introduce myself. I am your Average Guitar Joe, blithely living out the existence of a rock 'n' roll proletariat. Until recently, I was harboring a dark and terrible secret. I was a computer idiot, a walking anachronism who didn't know software from footware or floppy discs from a hole in the ground. Us guitar players, no matter what we claim, are still essentially affixed to the wild west mythos: Outlaws flauntin' a hot piece they ain't ascared to use iffen they hafta. Somehow, it's hard to play the same role armed with a pc terminal.

But stubborn pride gave way under intimidation from my editors. I had my first close encounter with a computer—and I not only survived with my psyche intact, but became a convert. If you've got my ailment, repeat after me ... *I am a computer idiot. I am a computer idiot. I am a computer idiot*. Good. Help is on its way. Take it from me; I was blind but now I see.

My own personal tourguide to computer awareness was MusicData. Presently an unassuming image on the third floor of the old Wilshire Theatre building on the edge of Beverly Hills, the company was born when synthesist Lance Ong met marketing wizard Ron Wilkerson at N.A.M.M. show. The company's first endeavors were along the lines of data cassettes programmed by big names to expand your stock synth sounds shipped from the factory. Music-Data's next logical step was toward software that serves as a bridge—not only between the synth and computer manufacturers, but between all that technological sophistry and Average Joe/Janes like me.

Lance Ong and technical partner Jeff Burger sat me down at the screen with a bit of cheerleading: "From a compositional standpoint, computers are a god-send," Ong states flatly. And given the organizational latitude of the sequencer, song assembly takes on an eerie mutability. The program is ideally suited to the art of pop songcraft. Pop songs, after all, are highly modular entities, sectional roadmaps of repeating verses, choruses and the odd bridge or coda. Aided by software, shifting parts around is as easy as punching the right key—no razor or splicing tape required. What better way to road test this new-fangled gadgetry than by rolling up the sleeves and digging in (without getting my fingernails dirty, of course). I was the perfect, innocent, guitar-based subject, armed only with a riff and a prayer. The odds got a bit stiffer when I found out that I wouldn't be able to use a Roland guitar controller to input the musical parts; I would have to tap my threadbare keyboard abilities on this perilous journey. Cold fear gripped me as I booted the disk and peered at my first menu. But when the going gets tough ...

I intentionally started with only a single four-bar funk riff in mind; I wanted to see what kind of creativity these babies could spur on. I started the process by programming a LinnDrum beat, one of those unwittingly awkward grooves that a drummer would never think of, or care to (to further betray my naivete, this was my first hands-on experience with a Linn). It was drunken drums along the Mohawk.

Synched into the Commodore to provide a clock pulse (tempo variable from either the Linn or the keyboard), the Linn provided the foundation. Using a Yamaha DX7 as my inputting keyboard, I next laid down the central riff with a slap bass sound, slowing down the tempo to suit my sluggard fingers. Only four bars of clean execution were needed, after which a one-note trigger on the next downbeat would seal off a loop. Many

9

takes later, my misbehaving digits pulled it off, and I got a taste of one of the large advantages of recording with the system: there is virtually no rewind time, because you're not rewinding.

Playing back the riff, I accidentally changed the DX7 patch to a log drum-sounding *marimbone. Eureka, an inspired flub!* The figure was too busy as a bass line anyway. So it was time to go back and put down a real, pithy bass part—something meaty and to the syncopated point. It was all sounding too linear, this complement of cycling loops, so I added a few simple chords to the stew, but quickly ran afoul a basic problem. The computer is an exacting stenographer, needless to say, and I had trouble telling it to violate barlines and to anticipate the downbeat without throwing the groove out of phase. Also, the prior loops had to fit into the longest loop evenly; I had a two-bar phrase, a four-bar phrase and a three-bar phrase, which adds up to *Help, Mr. Wizard!*

Getting around on a computer-generated sequencer, like the Los Angeles freeway system, requires some forethought. Computers, unlike live engineers, thrive on commands. They never take coffee breaks, it's true, but they also will never second-guess a musician in creative midstream. Get to know your downbeat. You don't have quite the fix-it-in-the-mix safety net where software is concerned. With MusicData's sequencing program, you check your status—which track is being engaged, tempo, transposition position, outgoing assignment (which track is triggering which synth in the playback) and an easy-to-read chart of sequence order—all on one screen at one time. An idiot's delight. You can squeeze a lot of musical substance out of scant actual ideas. For instance, I had set up my A section—a nice enough, bubbling ditty with a total of maybe thirty seconds playing time.

I then makeshifted a B section by instructing the Commodore to transpose everything but the bass up a fifth and swapped sounds. A Casio CZ-101 played the bass, the DX7 played *Marimbone* and an Oberheim OB-8 offered a brass sound, the latter two trading sounds between sequences of the tune. To give the illusion of musical direction, I cooked up another bass riff with an interlocking motif as a C section and played an actual solo, recorded at maybe two-thirds the eventual tempo. Getting the hang of this arrangements-while-you-wait enterprise, I plotted the different sections in a carefully random fashion on the sequence chart. As a sort of coda, I had the bass transpose down a fourth, reaching a sad and wonderful harmonic resolution that sends listeners pondering the whole art versus technology issue, or dinner.

Shockingly, my little untrained foray into the software resulted in a five-minute piece that bears an uncanny resemblance to music. It will never wend its way to vinyl, but this etude, which I humbly call "Blinded Me With Parlance," has a quirky, perky charm; it's an example of neo-expressionist, post-Jazzercise dogma. Available through modem only.

Most of all, my cassette copy of the tune acts as a verification of a rite of passage. I communed with a Commodore and found that we are not nemeses, that we could more than just peacefully coexist. In fact, the ease of musical operations afforded through computers raises a nasty question; will data-processing, by making musicians sound better than they actually are, erode the standards of modern musicianship? Is the computer musician a more indolent sort than his/her acoustic/analog ancestor? And will computers alter the way music is constructed and absorbed, resulting in more sterile, programmatic pragmatics, a more paint-by-the-number creative aesthetic? Will it change the contours of our thought patterns; is it apparent, for example, by the nature of my sentences that this manuscript was pecked on a rickety Smith Corona, when all about me have graduated to word processors? What's it all about, Apple?

One thing is certain; data is decidedly habit-forming and can lead to harder software pursuits. Computers are a behemoth inevitability and, as with the advent of existentialism, rock 'n' roll and nuclear warfare (not necessarily in that order), there's no turning back. Only now, that I've been ordained as a *user*, can I begin to sense the magnitude of this thing. Won't you join me?

Joe Zawinul

Weather Report's Fearless Leader Considers a Solo Flight Via MIDI Airways

By Josef Woodard

MUSICIAN: *I should begin by asking about the status of Weather Report as a musical entity. There's been talk of solo projects in the works.*

ZAWINUL: In all, I've got 2,000 pieces of music which I've done nothing with. If we keep on going like we've been doing, in other words, making records—as well as they might be—and touring all the time, we will be sixty-two and by that time I'm going to have 5,000 pieces of music and it is dead.

Let's say Weather Report is a hobby we can no longer afford to continuously *just* do. There are other things at this stage of our lives and we have to branch out. I think we made a great record, but I think we finally can afford to do something we want to do. Wayne hasn't done a solo album in eleven years. I haven't done one in sixteen years. He's in the studio right now. I'm also in the studio ready for a solo project. I'm still going to make records with Weather Report; however, momentarily, we will not travel with the band. I'll go out in the summer to Europe for four weeks by myself—just me and my synthesizers. That's something I've wanted to do for many years, and if I don't do it now, I ain't gonna do it. And now the technologies are such that I can go out as a full orchestra by myself.

MUSICIAN: *You basically want to get some creative skeletons out of the closet?*

ZAWINUL: Whatever the term is, it is something that has been waiting too long. And this is wonderful that it can be at home. Most people cannot do this. I don't have to be away from my family to make a living, which is great. If you want to do something right, man, you gotta take time, even if you're talented and you got your shit together. You gotta live with it. You gotta weigh everything.

For this solo album, I have about fifty or fifty-five songs. I don't know what to do with them, which ones to take and

"Now MIDI technology is such that I can go out on the road as a full orchestra by myself."

how to crystallize all this chaos. That's how it was on *Sportin' Life*. I'd just gotten my MIDI setup. The last song ("Ice-Pick Willy") was the first song I ever played with MIDI. The only thing that was done was editing, and Wayne overdubbed, Omar overdubbed the cymbal and I added the voices at the end and that's it. I personally didn't do any overdubs.

Same thing with "Indiscretions." "Hot Cargo" was totally on MIDI; the only overdubs were Wayne on the melody and Mino on the Simmons drums. This is the way to do it; it is inexpensive and it is totally spontaneous, towards total improvisation. That's what it's all about. We went through so many music, sheets of music, and out of all this, something crystallizes.

MUSICIAN: *So is it safe to say that there will be a good deal of keyboard layering on your album?*

ZAWINUL: Not so many layers, because the way I'm set up, I pretty much do everything in one shot. Like on this new album, there is no harmony or keyboard overdubs. It's done with MIDI; I play with one keyboard and they all do it in one shot, boom.

MUSICIAN: *Is it a matter of stretching the limits of what you already know?*

ZAWINUL: Well, I would be bored, man. I work every day on this stuff, and I have fun doing it. It is not that I say, "Today I'm going to work." For me, it's the greatest fun. I go in and fool around with my instruments and program in new sounds.

Everytime I find a new sound, I have a new song. Sound is composition, in other words. *Sound*. So, naturally, if you write every piece from the same sound, after a while it's going to be the same piece.

You hear all this stuff about the acoustic piano; I have nothing against the acoustic piano. It's as beautiful an instrument as any. But by itself, it's like potatoes. I love potatoes, man. But if you had to eat potatoes morning, mid-day and evening, there'd be fucking potatoes growing out of your ears. You don't want that to happen.

Sportin' Synths

Though Zawinul is lunging headlong into the MIDI orbit, he still swears by such ancient "relics" as an ARP analog sequencer (which his keyboard tech man **Jim Swanson** calls "the hippest analog sequencer ever devised") and a Prophet 5 as well as an Oberheim OB 8-voice both dating back longer than four years. "Joe is not a pure synthesist, who will say, 'I'm going to take this wavelength and form it this way. He tells me, 'I want this kind of sound,' so I'll roughly get it in the ballpark and he'll take over, tweek and fine tune it from there. That way he's not restricted to set patterns of working. It's the Eureka method—'Wow, this is nice, let's record that.'"

This season, Zawinul's keys consist of the following: A Sequential Circuits T8, Rhodes Chroma, an Ultimate Support rack holding a Korg DW6000 and a Prophet 5 equipped with MIDI, an Oberheim OB 8-voice and an Emulator, aided and abetted by a Linn LN-1 drum machine and an Oberheim Xpander module. His sequencers include the ARP as well as a Sequential Poly sequencer and Swanson's Oberheim DSX, equipped with Jim Cooper's MIDI-adaping Oberface. Swanson's self-designed MIDI switcher box will enable Zawinul extensive inter-keyboard flexibility. Also, a set of Korg MIDI pedals will ensure that none of Zawinul's limbs lie down on the job. "He can play a sampled drum set sound on the Emulator with the pedals," speculates Swanson.

One prospective Zawinul acquisition will be an IBM computer with Roland MPS composing software, which, with MIDI's help, can provide Zawinul—the improvising composer—with goofproof transcription of his ideas.

Michael McDonald

Hitmaking in the Garage: MIDI Makes a Pop Legend Leaner and Meaner.

By Josef Woodard

Don't talk about historical vindication or aesthetic politics with Michael McDonald; he's too busy working. It's not that he doesn't understand his heritage, or the extreme irony of the past eight years which has seen the punk movement first spit at the R&B-infected sophisto-pop of west coast bands like the Doobie Brothers only to adopt its synth-soul textures in more recent years. Nor is he unaware of the enduring compound of elements comprising his bleached gospel style. It's just that, when all is said and done, he'd rather do it than say it.

There's nothing pretentious or overwrought about the infectious material on *No Lookin' Back*, McDonald's second solo album and his first in three years. The tracks, all painted in shades of R&B and unabashedly pop hook-baiting, are most remarkable, in fact, for their directness, sparseness and clarity. Subtle deployment of MIDI'd synths are counterbalanced by the fleshy clutch of the Jeff Porcaro/Willie Weeks rhythm section and by pointed cameos from Cornelius Bumpus' sax and Robben Ford's guitar. With less extra-lyrical riffing than on almost any previous record, McDonald's voice nonetheless conveys a palpable essence of soul and affirmation. Move directly past the self-help pep song of the title cut—the album's first single—and listen to the control and vulnerability wrestling for power as he sings "Bad Times" or "Any Foolish Thing." The McDonald touch is fully engaged. Without catering to Hollywood pop glitter or to any imported haircut-of-the-month club, McDonald has made an archetypically *fine* pop record, easily among the year's best.

MIDI allowed McDonald to build from sparse basic tracks for more overdub decisions and greater clarity.

These days, he maintains two homes; one is a lush plot in Santa Barbara, the other an unassuming tract house in North Hollywood, in which the garage has been fully transformed into a 24-track studio. Most of *No Lookin' Back* was recorded here in his back yard, as well as some tracking at Jeff Porcaro's home studio across town. With his cachet of hair going from pepper to salt and his eyes like hotpools of blue, exuding sincerity, McDonald is a modest, readily likeable pop star. You believe him. This ain't mere show biz.

MUSICIAN: *On the new album, the byword is compactness. The tunes are tightly structured—not much solo space.*

MCDONALD: Not a lot of instruments, either, not nearly as much as you're used to hearing with this kind of stuff. Basically, we had always started off with more instruments. Cutting the basic tracks live, we always wanted to make sure we were covered and we had fairly good-sized rhythm sections to begin with. The overdubs were little things, touches, details. But on this new album, the basic tracks were the smallest parts—usually one synth and a drum machine—and the overdubs were everything. It was really working in reverse. It gives you a lot of leeway to make decisions. It can cost you more time in the process, but if you have a home studio like this, the initial expense is the bulk of it. We do what we can not to make a project a financial burden. You're not sitting around paying $200 an hour, so you take that time. It makes for a better record.

MUSICIAN: *I was somewhat surprised at how many acoustic instruments you do use. Given your talents and drawing on MIDI technology, it could have been a one-man album.*

MCDONALD: It could have been. I just don't feel that I play all that well that I'd *want* to do a one-man album. Also, too, I had a phobia about doing a totally synthesized record, full of synth timbres. One thing I noticed on the demos, which were primarily all synthesizers and drum machines, was that every time we put a real cymbal or something on it, it sounded beautiful. You'd be fooled into thinking that you had the whole spectrum covered with synths, but the minute you put something acoustic in the middle of those synths, they couldn't compare to the beauty of a real sound; they somehow didn't have the real ambience, the real life that Jeff Porcaro had when he cracked his snare in a room. But it was fun, because we did the album basically here and at Jeff's. The only thing we went out for was to mix.

MUSICIAN: *Home studios have a stigma: you're not supposed to be able to record a major album in one.*

MCDONALD: Yeah, but people have been doing it for quite a while—Gary Wright, a lot of people. The fact that I've done it *is* probably amazing. Technology's just not my bag. I've always approached it at arm's length, which was another reason I liked hearing real bass and real drums. It made the track sound more human. I don't care how well you deal with technology, after a whole album of it, you have to take it in that context and give up certain things I wasn't prepared to give up. I wanted things to have a little more emotion than machines could come across with.

MUSICIAN: *Is it hard to focus on one tune at a time, to finish it in one sitting?*

MCDONALD: It is. Writing is one of those things I've come to love and hate, and sometimes I hate it more than I love it, in all honesty. It's a horrible experience for me in a lot of ways, because I just get crazy. I don't know why; I second-guess myself a whole lot when I'm writing. And I think, in a warped kind of way, it makes your stuff better. I work slower than a lot of people and I put myself through a lot of changes.

With this record, the only part that was really tense—the usual bloodbath that record-making is about—was the writing part of it. I just couldn't be happy enough with the stuff. I really wanted to make sure that this record wasn't anything short of the best I could do at this time, a solid collection. I wasn't going to try to take ten years doing it or make a lifetime project out of it. But it did have to have a certain solidity, and validity to it. I love [Phil Collins'] *Face Value* album in that I can listen to the whole album, instead of just two cuts over and over again. I wanted to get somewhere in that realm.

McDonald's Arsenal

McDonald's main axe of choice for the past few years has been the Yamaha DX7. In working on the demos for *No Lookin' Back*, McDonald linked two DX7s via MIDI, and annexed an Emulator II and Roland Super Jupiter when seeking out the killer horn sound. He also uses a LinnDrum and a Yamaha QX1, which he calls "probably the best digital sequencer available." In the McDonald home studio/drawing board, we find an APF board, 3M tape decks, an Ampex 2-track and Yamaha cassette decks. As for outboard gear, he uses a Yamaha Rev 1 and Massenburg components, and dbx 160 compressor/limiters, but he has a special fondness for his Quantec Room Simulator. His trademark vocal mike is a Sennheiser; his studio mike is an AKG C-12.

Frank Serafine

Frankie Goes to Hollywood: A Top Sound Designer Finds MIDI Makes It Easier.

By Craig Anderton

These days Hollywood's hottest sound designer is an enthusiastic musician in his early thirties named Frank Serafine (pronounced Sehr-ah-*fee*-nee). Already under his belt are *Star Trek–The Motion Picture, Tron, Ice Pirates, The Fog, The Sword and the Sorcerer, Star Trek III, The Day After,* and a number of commercials. For Frank, being a musician was one of his strongest assets in getting gigs; the fine line between sound and music ceases to exist in Serafine's work. To him, putting a sound behind a scene in a movie is more than just plugging in a noise—it's equally important to have the right phrasing, timbre and emotional impact. I was surprised, for example, to find out that the bomb blasts in *The Day After* had a slowed-down lion's roar mixed in very prominently with the actual sound of the ex-plosion, and that the human screams were supplemented by pig screams. The disk tosses in *Tron* were a mix of pro-cessed bullwhip sounds and monkey screams. And in *Star Trek–The Motion Picture*, at one point the Enterprise was going into a black hole accompanied by the sounds of a barroom brawl played backwards (although purists could argue that there's no sound in space). How does Frank make those connections?

"Sometimes it's obvious what's needed. In *Star Trek III*, the sound effects supervisors and Leonard [director Nimoy] requested a sound representing major amounts of debris, and I knew at that point I had to get a bunch of metal debris and process it or whatever to make it fit into the picture. I ended up going to a junkyard and having stuff thrown around.

"As to how I chose the backwards barroom scene, it was

mostly experimentation...you pull things out of the library and start messing around with them. In this case physics gives you a clue; a metal bang or explosion turned backwards creates a suction feeling. Since the barroom brawl had a lot of bangs and hits and crashes, it created the perfect effect."

Gathering the sonic "raw materials" for the library is another matter altogether. Frank almost always uses a portable VCR and Sony PCM-F1 digital audio adapter for his field recording. The F1 converts audio into a wide-bandwidth signal suitable for recording on the VCR's video tracks; the sound quality is rivalled only by devices such as the Compact Disc.

Recording sounds is not easy. You might think that if you wanted a jet airplane, no problem; after all, you just go out to the airport and...."The problem with recording airplanes," says Frank, "is that if it's during the day, you'll pick up birds, or a dog barking in the distance; if it's at night, you have crickets to contend with. The way I finally got some good planes was over the Christmas holidays in Colorado, when there was a blanket of snow on the ground. There were lots of planes flying in, the snow absorbed any ambient sounds, and there weren't any crickets." And speaking of recording crickets, Frank has a tip: "Go to the pet store and buy a couple of crickets, then put them in a shoe box. Record them digitally, then multitrack them."

However, Frank does not deal exclusively with real-world sounds by any means, and music and MIDI are an important part of his act.

"I like to close the studio door when I'm creating; I do things when I'm by myself that I wouldn't do when other people are around. Music is a very intimate art form, and that's why MIDI is so incredible. It lets me have a bass player, drummer, guitarist and multiple keyboard players on call, yet I'm the only one who has to operate this stuff. I think being a one-person band is an elevating experience beyond belief. Once people figure out what MIDI can really do, the results will be revolutionary...it's beyond human comprehension right now. Let's face it, MIDI has really only been here one year. We're the pioneers in this."

Frank sees a future there with fewer session players, and more music done via MIDI by producers and the artists themselves. He elaborates: "I think for the most part this is due to economics—if something can be done better and cheaper, people are going to go that way. Creatively it's phenomenal too. One of the problems I always had with musicians is that they were always so moody, they were never there on time, stuff had to be set up, and in the studio time equals money. When you're dealing with egos and personalities and schedules, it's a stressful job. I don't have to worry about someone being on time anymore, or about where to put the mike on the bass drum.

"I think the future is in the MIDI studio. People will work out their tunes at home on a little MIDIfied Casio or whatever, or maybe even use portable equipment and compose stuff while traveling. After you have your tunes worked out, you bring your sequencer disc into a studio that has twenty-four MIDI synthesizers rather than twenty-four analog tracks, play back your sequences, and mix the whole thing down to digital. That's the future."

"Being a one-person band is an elevating experience beyond belief. That's why MIDI's so incredible."

Sounds good, but wouldn't that require that a composer be very familiar with all the characteristics of the synthesizers being MIDI'd? What if you work out a bass part with a particular synth in mind, then find that the studio doesn't have that synth available? As it so happens, Frank considers this an advantage, not a problem. "That's the amazing thing about MIDI—it can be full of surprises. Like you can write a composition around a koto sound, but if you try running through an instrument's presets you might find that marimba works better than koto. Or blending two sounds might be best of all. What I like most about MIDI is that it can go beyond what you can think of—once that sequence starts rolling, all you have to do is start pushing buttons and your composition will do things you hadn't anticipated or expected."

Frank treats MIDI as an "intelligent interface" between his various electronic instruments and uses SMPTE as the master timing reference for his studio. He records SMPTE time code on track sixteen of his 16-track Tascam, then records a MIDI-compatible sync track on track fifteen. Because the two sync signals "co-habitate" on the tape, they always maintain proper timing with respect to each other: SMPTE keeps the audio tape in sync with the video, and MIDI keeps the instruments in sync with the MIDI code. This may not be as elegant as using a single time code track and feeding it into a "black box" (like the Synchronous Technologies SMPL System, Roland SBX-80, or Garfield Master Beat) to derive sync from a master track, but his system works and works well. The Passport MIDI/8 sequencer, connected to an Apple II computer via the Passport interface, is the heart of Frank's MIDI setup.

Frank's keyboards include an E-mu Emulator, MIDIfied SCI Prophet 5 (Rev.2, or "the one with the good sound" as Frank says), Minimoog, Yamaha DX7, and Fender Rhodes. Other devices include the Roland CXQ-100, DeltaLab DL-2 delay line with memory module, Audio/Digital TC-2 delay line, Audio + Design SCAMP rack, DeltaLab DL-5 "Harmonicomputer," Lexicon 224 digital reverb, EXR 3 "projector," Roland Vocoder, and Roland pitch-to-voltage converter.

When it comes to drum machines, Frank tends to rely on the E-mu Drumulator, modified to include a J.L. Cooper three-kit board so that he has access to Latin percussion, a "Simmons," and the standard Drumulator sound. He also likes the Yamaha RX-15, says the Linn 9000 is "a real nice box," and thinks that the Oberheim DMX is "probably the best-sounding of all of them."

Howard Jones

Things only get better for the first truly MIDI-based pop star

By Jon Young

There's something wrong here. Big kids are supposed to make those hard adult choices, not get everything they want. You can be popular, but don't count on it. You can be accessible, but it may be at the expense of substance. And you can play all the instruments yourself, but forget about good live performances and an ongoing supply of fresh musical ideas.

Howard Jones, however, is having his cake and eating it too, just about any way you cut it. His second chartworthy LP of electronic pop, *Dream Into Action*, which spawned the hit single "Things Can Only Get Better," showcases Jones' still-evolving gift for interfacing a variety of synths, not to mention more traditional instruments. Having evolved in just a few years from "a Fender Rhodes, one mono synth and a clapped-out old drum machine," Jones has for some time now used sequencers and MIDI as the heart of his one-man live show (he only recently added backing musicians).

Jones calls *Dream Into Action* a "more colorful, punchier record" than first LP *Human's Lib*. "The sound is bigger because we used sampling a lot more, and that gave me a greater variety of sounds. You can sample any sound you want. I sampled my voice and that was great fun, because we could create choral textures that are really emotive. We sampled recorders and pianos—we messed about with filters to make the pianos sound more like flutes. I wrote brass parts on emulated brass and then got a real brass section [TKO Horns] to play it, 'cause it sounds better."

For all that, do not—repeat, *do not*—call Jones a techno- or synth-musician. "You listen to something like 'Life In One

Day' and you don't think of it as synth music, do you?" he asks. "I'm a songwriter, and I dress up my songs with the most modern sounds I can find. But I also like traditional music and I want to have a link to the past as well. I can play all my songs on the piano, so I don't think of myself as high-tech."

By contrast, Jones observes, "I would definitely call Depeche Mode a synth band, in fact the only real synth band left." Lest there be any confusion, he adds quickly, "I love their music. They break new ground with their sounds."

To keep his material fresh, Jones varies the way he composes. "Sometimes I did the whole song at the piano and then saw if it stood up when I transferred it to other instruments. Sometimes I got all my machines going and wrote to the sound of the drum machine. Sometimes I took a single keyboard and wrote that way. I get different inspirations from different setups.

"I like to write sections of songs separately and decide later the best way to line them up on the sequencer."

"'No One Is To Blame' was written at the piano. I think that's obvious. For 'Assault And Battery' I wrote using all my machines at once. I set up several Drumulators and MIDI'd my keyboards to get a layered sound. I had two Yamaha

DX7s, a Prophet T8 and a Roland MSQ-700 all going at once."

In effect, Jones can create a song and its arrangement at the same time. "Yeah, the bare bones, anyway," he says. "Actually, I like to write sections of songs separately and decide later the best way to line them up."

Philosopher or technician, Jones does take great pride in the mechanics of his craft. "A recent article in Britain said that my onstage sound was so perfect that it must all be on tape. In a way that was an incredible compliment but it was also very upsetting. I've spent five years putting together all the things that make my live show and I definitely don't use tapes. My whole show is based around live performance."

Detailing his onstage operation, Jones explains, "The main brain is a Roland MSQ 700, which is a sequencer that I've programmed to play things you can't do with your fingers. It sets up a click track that Trevor [Morais, drummer] plays to. My brother Martin plays bass and I do the rest by hand.

"I've got a remote keyboard, a Yamaha KX5 that can be routed to play any of the other keyboards from anywhere onstage; it's radio-MIDI'd. I use a Roland Jupiter 8, Juno 60, SCI Prophet T8 and Pro One, an Emulator II, a Moog Prodigy (his first synth), two Yamaha DX7s and a TX8. For digital drums I have two E-mu Drumulators, a Roland TR-808, a Simmons SDS6 sequencer and a set of SDS7s. I also just got a Linn 9000—the variation you can get on that is incredible. For sampling, I also use an AMS 15-80S digital delay. The setup is complicated, but it produces quite a big sound."

The System

The Perils and Pleasures of Living on the High-Tech Frontier

By J.D. Considine

David Frank, the keyboardist and resident electronics expert with the System, is sitting in a record company office, describing his band's first live gig. "We got out there to play," he recalls, "and they said, 'Here's the System!' I pushed the button; 'one, two, three, four' and...nothing happened."

Singer Mic Murphy, sitting at the other end of the table, breaks up. "Well, something happened," continues Frank. "Everything went out of sync immediately. After like one beat, all of a sudden the drum machine was starting over again and the sequencers went nuts. It was unbelievable."

It was also especially ironic for a band so seemingly high-tech. By taking a name like the System, Frank and Murphy almost emphasize the synthesizers, sequencers and drum machines that contribute to their sound. Not that the band comes across as dance-floor automatons the way Kraftwerk sometimes does; indeed, the percolating bass patterns and sinuous synth lines Frank pulls from his gear give the System a decidedly human sound.

Nor has that humanizing touch gone unnoticed, for although the System has placed its name on only three albums, *Sweat, X-periment* and the recent *The Pleasure Seekers*, their sound has graced a host of outside projects. Starting with Robert Palmer's version of "You Are In My System," the System has contributed to such singles as Chaka Khan's "It's My Night," Scritti Politti's "Wood Beez" and Phil Collins' "Sussudio," and done production for artists ranging from soul crooner Howard Johnson to former Bow-Wow-Wow singer Annabella Lwin.

In fact, the two spend so much time in the studio, they seem almost to cherish their tales of trouble on tour. That, too, has its ironies, given that Frank and Murphy first teamed up while on the road with Kleer. But, as Murphy puts it, "One of the reasons we started producing records is that we're not a traditional soul act, and not being one, it's very difficult to accept dates doing soul tours. So our gig has been to do records in the studio."

Sometimes, it's an album, sometimes just odd jobs. Consider the case of "Sussudio." According to Frank, Phil Collins gave him the demo tape just to see what he could do with it. "The song wasn't going to be on the album at all, as a matter of fact," Frank says. "He just asked me to do something that would make him more interested in it. Everybody had reacted to the song by saying it sounded too much like '1999.' I'm not sure whether I made it sound any *less* like '1999,' but the bass line was not on the demo at all. The bass line and the whole thing was very different. The whole song had an eighth-note feel, and I made it a sixteenth-note feel. I decided that maybe that's what he wanted."

After-the-fact editing is an important System M.O.: "One of the by-products of having all these electronic instruments," comments Frank, "is that there have been many changes in musical style based on how easy it is to just turn the drum machine on and let it go, without changing anything. All of a sudden, people start to hear that a lot, they get used to hearing the high-hat play sixteenths through the whole song."

**"It's like a puzzle—you can actually put all different
possibilities in the sequencer and shift back and forth."**

"Having the programmability," adds Murphy, "you can change certain parts of it. You can say, okay, let's change bar four. It's like having a puzzle; you have the frame, and it's like you're filling in the pieces. It's really a unique way of doing it; you can actually put all different possibilities in the sequencer and shift back anc forth. You can truncate parts, and say, 'Let's use the chorus and half of the bridge.'"

Homework also plays a big part in the way the two record. "We might spend three days at home programming a song," says Frank. "We certainly wouldn't want to have done that in the studio without running the tape. At home, we're just sitting there thinking, 'Is this a nice combination of sounds?' It saves a lot of time in the studio, and it makes us feel a lot better about going in there.

"Many times, Mic and I will sequence the whole song. 'My Radio Rocks,' we used the PPG Wave Term sequencer, and two Oberheim DSXs. Sequenced the entire song, did the drums, and basically came into the studio, plugged in about 59,000 outputs, and put it down all at once. On the one hand, we want to feel like we're going into the studio and are going to have some sort of adventure and be creative; on the other hand, we don't want to go in there with too little information, and then come out with nothing. So we try to keep a balance between what we've already done and what we have to do."

In addition to the DSX, the System uses an Oberheim OBX-a, Xpander and DMX drum machine, (with JL Cooper translator boxes to MIDIfy the pre-MIDI models). They also have a PPG Wave 2.3, a Yamaha DX7 and RX11, an Emulator II, a Minimoog, an Oxford synthesizer and a Simmons sound module. And to make sure that their live show is never again scrambled by the power spike they later discovered was at fault for their debut fiasco, they now take a rechargeable industrial 110-volt storage battery on tour for ultra-stable power.

Despite their ample collection, both Frank and Murphy cast a jaundiced eye upon the notion of more synths making better music. "I have my doubts if it's the number of synthesizers you have MIDI'd together that makes it sound better," gripes Murphy. "Sometimes if you just have one or two synthesizers MIDI'd together, you get a much harder sound than you would if you had six or seven. We tried one time to use the Yamaha TX816 rack, where you have eight DX7s." He turns to Frank. "Was it successful at all?"

"It sounded ridiculous," his partner answers. "We never ended up using all the modu es, because the sounds were totally overbearing. We'll find ourselves with too many synthesizers MIDI'd together, and all of a sudden, every sound has a little bit of bell, a little bit of analog, a little bit of digital. Pretty soon, all the parts begin to have the same dimension. "It's a danger that people get into. They get all this gear, and they use all of it. The most important thing is whether the melody, the chords and the feel of the song work together well, whether the little twists somewhere in the song work just right. After that, you just have to be more particular."

"And you know what?" adds Murphy. "The average knucklehead doesn't know the difference."

The MIDI Recording Studio.

How to Buy It, How to Set It Up, and How to Run It.
By Craig Anderton.

MIDI has received a lot of hype, but as more and more people are finding out, there is substance behind the hype. The MIDI sequencer has now made it possible to create an entirely different kind of recording studio for electronic music. As you play a melodic line on a MIDI keyboard, the computer-based sequencer "remembers" what you play and assigns this data to a track in the sequencer. You can build up multiple tracks, and on playback, send this musical data to multiple MIDI slave keyboards—thus producing the same effect as if you had multitracked the keyboards with a conventional multitrack tape recorder. This sequenced composition can then be mixed and recorded onto a conventional 2-track analog recorder, or (for maximum fidelity) PCM adapter/VCR combination to produce a master tape. Let's consider some of the advantages of this approach.

● First generation sound quality. What you hear on your final master is the sound of the MIDI instruments, with no intervening tape processes to degrade their clarity. With MIDI, the multitrack tape recorder is an option, not a necessity.

● No rewind time when working out compositions. Until the final mixdown, everything is stored in computer memory for virtually instant access.

● Zero fidelity loss when bouncing, no matter how many times you bounce. After all, you're bouncing computer data instead of sound.

● The ability to edit as little as one thirty-second note of one instrument on one track. Forget about the tortures of such techniques as the "window splice" (where, with tape, you splice a tiny window out of a multitrack tape to eliminate one bad note).

● Lower tape and maintenance costs. You don't have to align the bias or azimuth of a MIDI sequencer, or oil the motor, or worry about temperature and humidity extremes.

● Instantly change the sound of a track. Would that violin sound better as a trumpet? Punch a few buttons and find out; there's no need to do any re-recording.

● No noise reduction needed (unless you want to add some when you mix your multitracked composition over to a master tape).

● And even more amazing stuff you'll find out about during the course of this article. The MIDI recording studio is the most exciting development since inexpensive multitrack tape decks became available in the mid-70s. Don't sell your faithful multitrack recorder (yet); but if you were considering upgrading to sixteen or twenty-four tracks, you might want to reconsider. MIDI can help you upgrade your studio to a lot more tracks for a lot less bucks, so let's see exactly what the MIDI studio is all about.

MIDI Basics.

Many musicians think of MIDI solely as a way to get two keyboards to "talk" to each other. But MIDI goes beyond simple keyboard-to-keyboard hookups—think of MIDI as a *language* that conveys musical information such as pitch, duration of a note, dynamics of a note, what song you're playing, the current measure of a song you're playing, etc.

To understand the significance of this language, consider the player piano, which is conceptually very similar to a one-track MIDI recording studio. With the player piano, a paper roll contains data (the "words" of the player piano's language) concerning the notes of a composition; this data takes the form of little punched holes. Playing back this data into the player piano polyphonically activates appropriate key depressions, thereby providing a replica of the particular performance recorded (stored) in the paper roll.

MIDI presents a far more efficient way of creating pre-programmed compositions. First, instead of coding data on paper rolls, MIDI data is recorded in computer memory. This allows for much easier editing, since computer memory can be recorded and erased at will (try doing that with a paper roll!). Second, MIDI carries much more data than simply which notes are on and which are off, including dynamics and the other elements of the "language" we alluded to earlier. Third, MIDI lets you send out different data to different instruments over sixteen MIDI "channels": that's sixteen player pianos, playing their own individual polyphonic parts, and all being fed from one piano roll containing the score for all sixteen pianos.

In a standard instrument-to-instrument MIDI hookup, one instrument is the master and sends data out to a slave over the MIDI cable (see Figure 1). When the slave receives MIDI data from the master, it does whatever the master tells it to do—play a certain note, for a certain duration, etc. However, in the MIDI studio the master is usually not a keyboard, but a computer-based sequencer feeding multiple slave keyboards (we'll describe how to hook these together later). Using a computerized sequencer to control MIDI instruments is not as expensive as you might think; over the past few years, computer memory costs have declined to the point where you can store thousands and thousands of pieces of MIDI data in a very inexpensive computer. You could very easily base an "entry-level" MIDI studio around the Commodore 64, which sells for as low as $110.

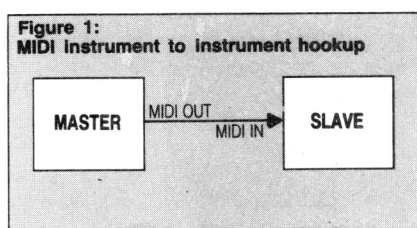

Figure 1:
MIDI instrument to instrument hookup

MASTER — MIDI OUT / MIDI IN → SLAVE

By now, the picture should be getting clearer. To recap, MIDI records not the *sound* of the notes you play, but *data* about which notes you play (up to sixteen channels' worth of data). If you feed that data back into an instrument, you have a high-tech equivalent of the player piano that faithfully duplicates what you originally played. The end result is like recording on tape, except that you have a lot more flexibility with a computer than you do with tape (or for that matter, punched paper).

Now let's consider the components that make up a MIDI studio, and what is involved in MIDI recording.

MIDI Instruments.

The first step in buying is to gather together some MIDI instruments; after all, these are what make the sounds. Your choice of instruments will largely be a matter of taste and budget, but I do have some suggestions.

A MIDI sampling keyboard is an expensive but important item. While sequencing all-electronic sounds can be very satisfying, adding in some "real-world" sounds gives you a much broader sonic palette. I've also found that doubling sampled sounds with synthetic sounds usually comes across more forcefully than either sound by itself. Even a relatively inexpensive instrument such as the Ensoniq Mirage (or the Decillionix sampling program hooked up to an Apple II) can do wonders, and naturally a high-tech instrument like the Emulator II or Kurzweil 250 can do proportionately more.

You will also want some kind of expander sound module. An expander is basically a synthesizer without the keyboard; it is accessed solely via MIDI. Because it doesn't have a keyboard, you can save some bucks compared to a standard keyboard instrument with equivalent capabilities. There are many good expander modules out on the market. I particularly like the Oberheim Xpander because the MIDI implementation is very complete, it sounds great, and it is far more flexible than the average synth. In the low-price category, Casio's CZ-101 mini-keyboard makes a fine expander module because no one else gives you such good-sounding voices for such little cost. And in the one-size-fits-all category, Yamaha's TX816, a rackful of DX7 expander modules, makes all those wonderful digital sounds which are all over the airwaves these days (doesn't anybody program their own sounds anymore?). Yamaha also recently introduced the TX7, an expander module version of the DX7. Roland makes a number of their products available in an expander box format, as does Korg, and some of Sequential's low-cost keyboards (like the Six-Trak and Max) make cost-effective MIDI expanders.

I'm particularly partial to expanders and keyboards that offer multitimbral capability. This lets you choose an individual timbre for *each voice* in the synthesizer, as well as assign each voice to its own MIDI channel. Thus, multitimbral instruments such as the Xpander or Six-Trak can give you six independent melody lines (one per voice).

Guitarists are not out of the picture by any means. Roland's GR-700 has a MIDI output that lets you interface one of the GR-series guitars to MIDI gear, and IVL, a Canadian company whose products are distributed in the U.S. by Cherry Lane, are as of this writing nearing completion on a polyphonic guitar-to-MIDI converter that has a target price of around $1,000. Top guitar makers like Gibson and Steinberger are adding new models with Roland circuitry aboard. Devices such as the Fairlight "Voicetracker" and IVL "Pitch Rider" even let vocalists, woodwind players,

and others program MIDI devices from their instruments. As you might expect, these tend to have more limitations than keyboards since non-electronic instruments are much harder to adapt to MIDI. As one example, the GR-700 cannot send pitch bend information over MIDI, but instead quantizes all notes in semitone steps. Also, there is a fair amount of processing lag as the GR-700's computer analyzes the string and converts this data to MIDI information. Still, most of these limitations are well worth working around in order to gain the advantages of interfacing traditional instruments with the MIDI studio; there's something about playing a sampled piano sound from a guitar that is really quite mind-boggling.

You'll also need a MIDI drum machine, hopefully one which responds to velocity information and song data (i.e. the drum unit automatically switches to the desired song upon command). Fortunately, though, many older non-MIDI drum machines will work with MIDI se-

This new Berklee College electronic music work station mixes all three sounds: analog (an Oberheim Xpander), sampling (Kurzweil 250) and digital (a Yamaha TX816 rack off-camera), plus digital drums (RX11).

quencers that can send out a drum-compatible clock pulse signal.

The most important point to remember for any MIDI instrument is that to be most effective in the MIDI studio, the instrument should have as complete a MIDI implementation as possible. You should at least be able to receive, and preferably transmit, on all sixteen channels. Being able to transmit a keyboard's velocity (dynamics) information over MIDI is also very important, because it lets you do your own "mix" as you play (velocity keyboards are also great for programming those MIDI drum units that accept dynamic information). Expander boxes need to be capable of receiving this velocity information and responding to it.

Program change over MIDI, where changing a "patch" on the master also causes a corresponding program change on slave instruments, is also convenient. Most MIDI instruments let you program them to either accept or ignore program changes. Program change can also function as a sort of pseudo-automated mixdown if you copy a patch over to several different program numbers that differ only in level: When you need a change, call up the program with the desired level.

Finally, the instrument controllers (pitch blend, modulation, breath controller, etc.) should be assignable to different MIDI controller numbers. (MIDI can send individual controller information for each basic channel.) Assignable controllers are great problem-solvers since there is no standardized correlation between controller number and function (except for pitch bend, which is MIDI controller 0, and sustain pedal, which follows a de facto standard of MIDI controller 64).

Once you have MIDI keyboards, a MIDI drum machine, and some expander modules, it's time to add the heart of the MIDI studio—a MIDI sequencer.

The MIDI Sequencer.

This has the same relationship to a MIDI studio as a multitrack tape recorder has to a conventional studio, and should be chosen with equal care. A good MIDI sequencer lets you do lots of tricks you can't do with a normal tape recorder. There are three types: the *add-on* sequencer for commercially available computers, the *built-in* that is part of a MIDI instrument, and the *stand-alone* which is conceptually closest to a tape recorder. Let's look at each type.

● **Add-on.** There is a seemingly endless stream of MIDI add-on sequencer programs: Waveform, Musicdata, Cherry Lane, Sight & Sound, Yamaha, Passport, Sequential, Roland, and a zillion others seem determined to get us using our home computers as sequencers. Whether you have an Apple, Commodore, or IBM computer (Atari will soon join the club), there's a MIDI sequencer for you. In addition to the software that tells the computer how to be a sequencer, most of these require some sort of hardware interface that hooks the computer up to a MIDI IN and MIDI OUT connector. The typical interface costs $100 to $200.

If you don't already have a personal computer, you might consider getting a built-in or stand-alone sequencer. Then again, computers are useful for lots of other purposes—you can't play games, create spreadsheets or do word processing on a MIDI keyboard...much less access an electronic bulletin board or meet a hot date. Choosing a computer for musical applications could be a whole article in itself, but here are some personal observations.

The IBM PC has some good MIDI software programs available, as well as bunches of business software. It is well-supported, but as a business machine it also has some problems (such as the inability to easily go multi-user). I also feel it's not particularly cost-effective, but I suppose you can get away with that kind of thing when you're IBM. If you do consider a PC, note that some of the IBM clone machines are generally acknowledged to be superior from a technical standpoint, yet cost less than IBM's offerings.

Yamaha's MSX-compatible CX5M is a decent "musician's computer" that is designed specifically to augment Yamaha equipment. It's not a bad computer at all, but is the least supported of all the computers mentioned so far because the MSX software standard has not had much of an impact in this country (most people I know haven't even heard of it). This could change if MSX software from Japan and Europe establishes a presence in this country.

Many musicians already have an Apple II or IIe, an extremely well-supported computer with thousands of available programs and add-on accessories (including much MIDI software). It's useful for business applications, makes an excellent home computer and is pretty inexpensive these days.

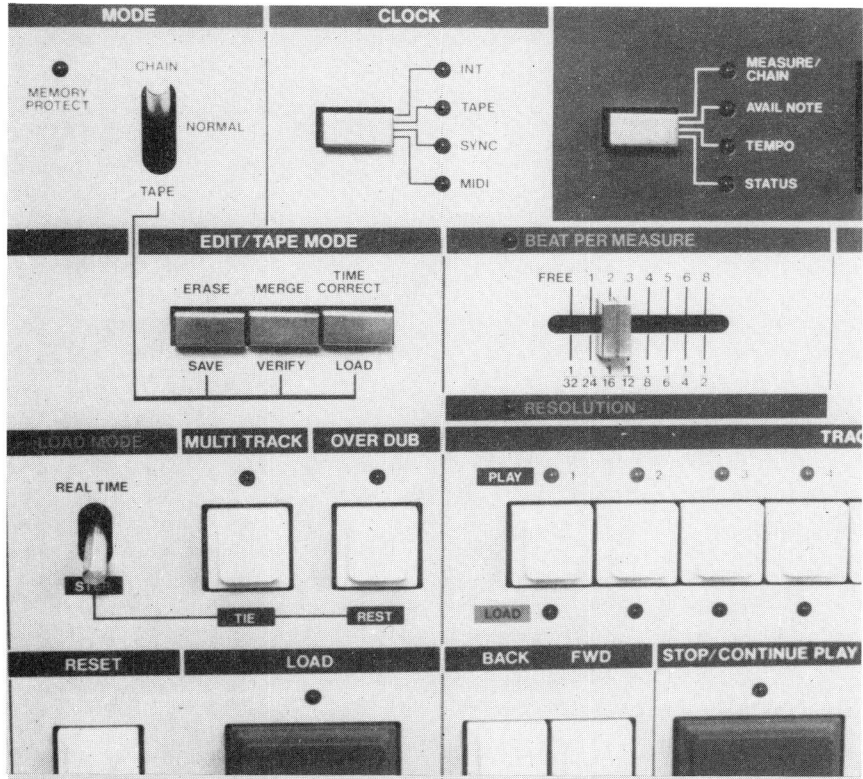

Front panel of a Roland MSQ-700 sequencer; notice how the transport buttons at the bottom resemble those of a conventional tape recorder.

Apple's Macintosh is rapidly becoming the "artist's favorite" due to its sleek packaging and the MacPaint program. Remarkable programs from several new companies are currently available and many more are on the way. Either of these computers is a good choice for a fairly serious personal computer. Commodore's new Amiga will also warrant a good look. You might also want to take into account that the Mac's graphic abilities, coupled with Apple's high-resolution laser printer, seem ideally suited for lead sheeting and transcription (once the software becomes available).

Commodore's C-64 is a wonderful game machine, it's inexpensive and there's lots of software, but it is also less "pro" than the machines mentioned above. However, for those on a budget the C-64 is an ideal way to get involved in MIDI recording. And when you upgrade to a better computer, you can always use the C-64 to play Zaxxon.

As of this writing Atari still has not introduced its line of new computers, all of which supposedly have provisions for MIDI. Atari is the dark horse of the industry, and has made a list of bold promises about the products it will be delivering over the next few months. If these promises come true, Atari should be a very strong contender in the MIDI sequencer sweepstakes. Also in the rumor category: Commodore's Amiga, which is supposed to be great but has yet to make any kind of substantive appearance.

● **Built-ins.** Sometimes sequencers are included as part of an instrument. E-mu's Emulator II, for example, includes a very complete eight-track MIDI sequencer. The Linn 9000 is another "MIDI-ready" device, which combines a high-tech drum machine with a sophisticated built-in MIDI sequencer. The OB-8, when retrofitted for MIDI, can send DSX sequencer info through the OB-8 MIDI OUT connector. The advantage of the built-in approach is less redundancy, while the disadvantage is less flexibility.

● **Stand-alones.** Yamaha's QX1 and the LinnSequencer or Linn 9000 are the first true, highly complete MIDI sequencers I've seen. These are the functional equivalent of a conventional multitrack recorder, right down to the "fast forward" and "rewind" buttons. I expect we'll be seeing more of these kinds of machines in the future. Roland's MSQ-700, while less sophisticated, is another very popular stand-alone sequencer.

No one sequencer can be all things to all musicians; the following list includes some of the most common and important features you can expect to find as you look at sequencers, and can serve as a check list when evaluating different models to see which one most closely meets your needs. Caution: As with synthesizers, not all manufacturers refer to a feature by the same name.

● Number of tracks. Sequencers typically come in 4-, 8-, 12- and 16-track versions. I've found eight to be adequate; I would feel differently, I'm sure, if I had sixteen MIDI keyboards.

● Reasonably complete MIDI implementation. The sequencer should be able to send note-on/off data plus dynamics as a bare minimum, and be capable of assigning any track to any channel; pitch wheel change, pressure change and program change are also very important.

● Programmable auto correct (also called quantization). While recording, auto correct rounds off timing errors in your playing to the nearest note value you specify—quarter notes, eighth notes, triplets, etc. Generally, a high resolution or real time mode will also be available so that you can defeat auto correct. Some sequencers auto correct

only during playback, which is a useful feature since you can change auto correct on an already recorded track.

● Disk storage option. This is a lot faster than saving data on cassettes, and more reliable too.

● Real-time, modular and step time programming. Real time lets you record like a tape recorder, where you put the sequencer into record and play away. Step time lets you move one-step-at-a-time through each and every step in the sequence, deleting or adding notes as you see fit. Some sequencers only let you do one or the other. Modular recording lets you create individual patterns which are then linked into songs (like drum machine programming). These patterns may usually be recorded in real time or step time. Note that step time, while useful, can often be simulated on real-time-only sequencers by simply slowing the tempo way down.

● Punch-in and punch-out. Careful, though; there are some subtleties to MIDI punching. If you punch right after a "note on" command and don't program anything to turn that note off, the original note will sustain in the background. A pre-roll feature is also handy, where you can program a section to start playing a couple of measures before the punch occurs.

● Programmable tempo changes. Being able to change the tempo for a song is very useful. Unlike tape, speeding up and slowing down a MIDI sequencer doesn't affect the timbre of the

Macintosh-based, four-pitch-wheel-drive MIDI studio: road test one today.

instruments. This makes it very easy to play complex parts at a slow speed, then boost the speed up for playback. Being able to program relative tempo changes—accelerando and ritardando—helps considerably to humanize a track.

• Track re-assignment. Maybe you want to drive your Mirage instead of your DX7 from track 5 without having to do any repatching; this option will let you do it.

• Easy commands. You want to do the least amount of typing necessary. A program which requires only single-letter commands and lets you move a cursor around to make selections is better than one which makes you type in stuff like "SAVE: COMPOSITION #1 IN B-MINOR: DISK A."

• Printout option. Some score/lead sheet printout programs are better than others, but just about all of them beat doing it by hand.

• Ability to name sequences and tracks. It's much easier to remember a song title than a number. Naming tracks is also handy; that way you know which instrument is driven by what track.

• Programmable countdown. I don't know about you, but I always need a few beats before a song starts in order to prepare myself for recording.

• Programmable metronome. Being able to program fast metronome times means that you'll still have a solid click reference if you slow the sequence way down when overdubbing.

• Expandable number of events. Most sequencers seem to be able to remember somewhere between 5,000 and 10,000 events (with note on, note off, pitch bend and so on being considered as "events"). This is fine for working on a song, but not always enough for a set of music. Being able to expand the memory to, say, 70,000 events with an optional memory expansion package leaves more space for sequences.

• Memory space status. You should be able to check how much memory is left.

• Readable manual. Make sure the person writing the manual is trying to instruct you, not impress you. If the first few pages make good sense, the rest probably will too.

• Sync-to-tape and external clock facilities. The ideal sequencer would be able to sync to anything—MIDI timing information, SMPTE click pulses and so on. Generally, sequencers don't have all these capabilities, although you can usually find a suitable adapter box (try J.L. Cooper, Roland, Garfield Electronics, Synchronous Technologies,

etc. for specific situations).

• Non-destructive editing. When editing a sequence, some sequencers create a copy which you edit. This preserves an unedited version of the original in case you end up not liking the edited sequence as much (don't you wish tape recorders would save a previous track when you did an overdub?) Once you get an edited version you prefer, then over-write the original.

• Fast forward/rewind. It's fun to hear the sequence whiz by as you look for a part towards the beginning or end of a song.

• Search. Search looks for a particular part of the sequence, or places you a certain number of measures into it.

• Bounce. You should be able to bounce around data for tracks, and combine tracks together (thus, you could play sections of a complex part for one instrument on several tracks, then bounce them all down to create on composite part on one track).

• Transpose. So you can't sing that song in D# after all? Then transpose until you hit the right range.

• Filter. I first saw this used in Roger Powell's "Texture" program to selectively eliminate data from a track. For example, suppose you played left and right hand parts on a single keyboard, and wanted to split off the left hand part to a different keyboard. You could copy the track and filter the low notes from the original, thus sending the right hand

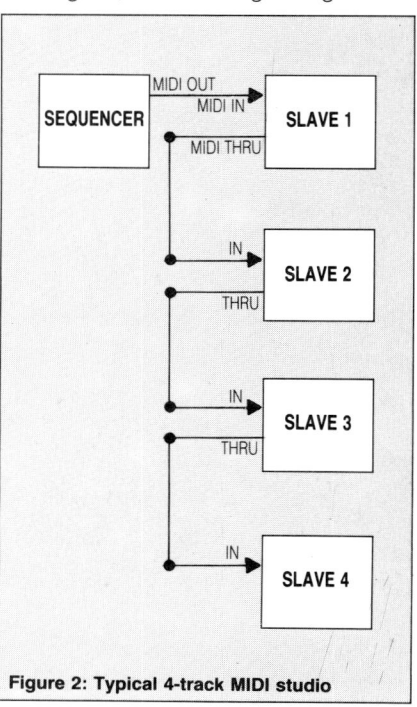

Figure 2: Typical 4-track MIDI studio

part to one instrument; then, you could filter the high notes from the copy and send the low notes (the left hand part) to a different instrument.

● Mute/cue function. This lets you selectively silence tracks while recording. One use is to record four or five different solos, and listen to each one individually. For live use, this means you can play different solos at different performances so you don't get bored with hearing the same sequenced part over and over and over and over again.

● Free software updates. According to Anderton's Law of High-Tech Equipment Purchasing, never buy anything that says "Version 1.0" unless the company will upgrade you to the next software revision for free. Initial software offerings often have bugs; by the time you get to version 1.4 or so, the bugs are pretty much all gone.

Hooking It All Up.

Now we have our tools together, so let's hook everything up. **Figure 2** shows a typical setup for a four-track MIDI studio. The MIDI signal from the computer interface or sequencer goes to Slave #1's MIDI IN. A replica of the signal entering Slave #1's MIDI IN is available at the MIDI THRU connector (sort of like the "dry out" or "direct out" found in effects boxes), which we use to send the computer data to Slave #2. By feeding MIDI THRU jacks to MIDI IN jacks, we can send the computer data to several slaves.

However, as we all know MIDI is not perfect; some instruments do not provide MIDI THRU jacks, and in any event, this way of interconnecting devices only works for a limited number of keyboards (as the MIDI signal goes through multiple THRU outputs, it can be the victim of "data distortion" due to technical limitations of the MIDI interface). **Figure 3** shows the solution: Use a MIDI THRU accessory box, which provides an individual MIDI OUT signal for each instrument. Each MIDI OUT connects to the instrument's MIDI IN jack. Several companies make MIDI THRU boxes with four to eight outputs; for those who really want to stretch their studio, Synchronous Technologies markets a 16-channel MIDI THRU box.

Using It.

Congratulations! Everything is in place and ready to go. Dig out the sequencer's owner manual and start putting it through its paces. Remember to set your MIDI channels and modes (omni-poly-mono) correctly, and you're off.

Not everything will go smoothly, of

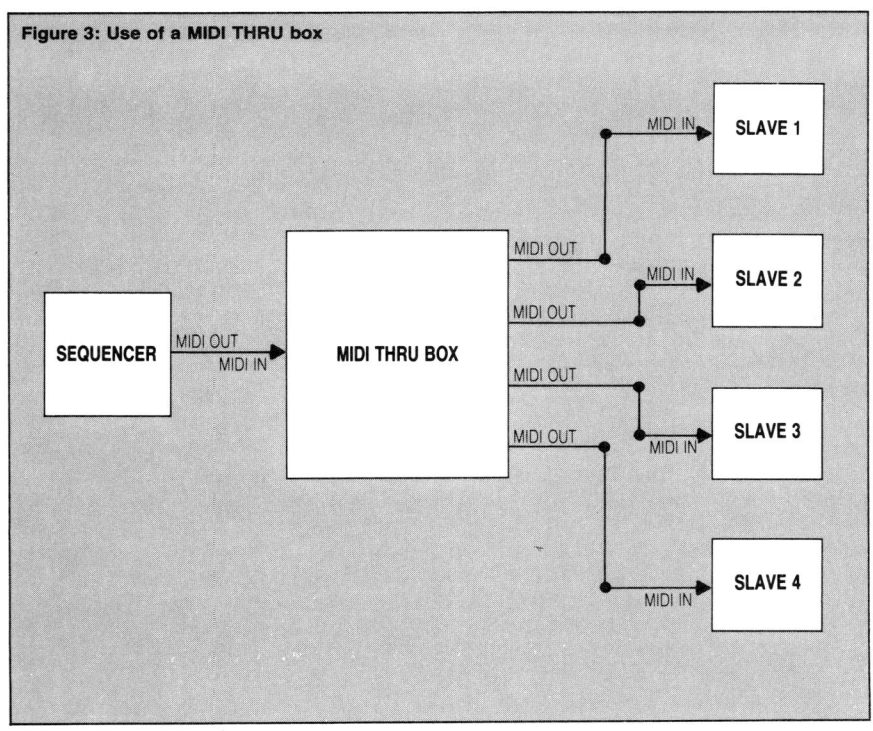

Figure 3: Use of a MIDI THRU box

course. You should be prepared for surprises (both good and bad), and some frustration. Remember those times your tape recorder wouldn't record—until you noticed that you were in sync mode? Those kinds of "beginner's mistakes" are very common when using MIDI. MIDI has so many variables that things seldom work perfectly from the beginning. You will have to make sure that your controllers are set so that they can talk to the sequencer, and you might occasionally run into a hardware or software bug. These are part of the deal, just like a drop-out on regular tape. The important thing is not to give up, or let frustration take the upper hand. Come back later with a fresh outlook, study the manual a little further and experiment.

Once you begin to use the MIDI studio, you'll really start to appreciate how much it simplifies and speeds up the composition process. For years, I've been waiting for the tapeless studio, and it's finally here. If you've been looking for something truly new in musical electronics, this is it...recording will never be the same again.

MIDI Protocol: the Diplomacy of Digital.

How Musical Nations of Many Languages Do Business Together.
By Alan di Perna.

Only a computer could count all the words that have been written about MIDI over the past year or so. And if computers could quantize the emotional tone behind these words, there'd be high readings in the category labelled "Awestruck Wonderment". We've had countless reports on hot new MIDI products and fervent claims that, by the end of the decade, MIDI will have landed your DX7 on Mars and established an intergalactic network of home studio satellites.

It's easy to get carried away speculating on the long-term possibilities of MIDI. But this article's on a much more mundane mission. We're here to seek out and explore the MIDI protocol itself; to boldly cut through marketing hype and the murky mire of in-group tech talk; to emerge, eyes triumphantly alight, with a clear understanding of the vast reaches just beyond that mystifying acronym we mortals call MIDI.

What's in the Wire? As we all know, MIDI (the Musical Instrument Digital Interface) is a computer interface devised by five top synth manufacturers (Sequential, Roland, Yamaha, Korg and Kawai). It's specifically designed to work with the kind of microprocessors you find in synthesizers, drum machines and sequencers, and to interface these with appropriately equipped microcomputers. The data is transmitted from one device to another via patterns of electronic blips that travel through the specially-designed MIDI cable.

The exact form and content of this data are all laid out in the MIDI Specification 1.0, which is the Holy Writ for any manufacturer who wants to create a MIDI product. Anyone may read the text, though. It's available for a nominal fee from the International MIDI Association (11857 Hartsook St., North Hollywood, CA 91607 [818] 505-8964). The IMA, in fact, has just brought out an expanded, more detailed version of the MIDI Spec —a sort of Revised Standard Version. It doesn't change anything that's in the original MIDI Specification; it just fills in some of the "gray areas". (More on this later.)

So what does the 1.0 Specification have to say about MIDI data? Well first of all, we learn that the data is organized into packets of information known as bytes. The bytes are made up of electronic blips called bits. There are eight data bits in a MIDI byte, plus a start bit and a stop bit. The start and stop bits are there to enable the microprocessors to distinguish between the end of one byte and the beginning of the next. Remember, all we're dealing with here is a line of blips coming down a wire, so it must be made clear which blips belong to which blip family in order for the MIDI message to make sense. The "language" of computers, you see, is binary arithmetic, a system where the only values are 0 and 1. When the current is on, that signifies a logical 0 in MIDI; current off equals a logical 1. Each byte, then, is a packet of 0s and 1s arranged in different combinations, each of which carries a different message.

The MIDI Spec goes on to distinguish between two different types of byte. Status bytes identify what kind of information is being transmitted. These guys come down the line first, and say things like, "I'm telling you to turn a note on," "I'm telling you to do a pitch bend," or "I'm telling you to change from one patch preset to another." Close on the tail of the status byte comes one or more data bytes. These furnish the particulars: "The note I want you to play is Middle C. Play it with X amount of attack velocity." If the receiving instrument is configured to perform all of these specific tasks, it will do so. If not—say it's a keyboard synth that doesn't have velocity sensitivity—it will respond to those commands it can carry out (in this example, it will play Middle C) and ignore the commands it can't carry out (in this case, the velocity information).

In saying this, we've dispelled the First Great MIDI Misconception: that connecting a less sophisticated synthesizer to a more sophisticated machine will give the economy model all the performance features of the deluxe job. It just doesn't happen that way.

Are You Picking Up Now? MIDI is set up so that information can be transmitted and received over sixteen different channels. This is what lets you play one-man band and have a MIDI sequencer (or personal computer/MIDI software setup) controlling a whole roomful of instruments, each playing a different part, all in perfect sync. Each instrument can "tune in" to the channel that carries the part it should play. At the same time, all the channels can share certain common types of data, which enables all the instruments to synchronize and coordinate what they're doing. Thus the MIDI Specification, in its infinite wisdom, distinguishes between two basic types of MIDI message: Channel Messages and System Messages.

Channel Messages: In the status byte of a channel message, the first four bits (collectively known as a "nibble" in cutesy computerese) address the message specifically to one of the sixteen channels. Only those instruments which are "tuned in" to that channel will respond to the message. The remaining four bits of the status byte go on to specify the type of data that will follow.

System Messages: These messages are *not* encoded with channel numbers and are subdivided into three types:

1. *System common* messages go out to all units on all channels in any given MIDI hookup. These are the MIDI messages with a sense of place. They make it possible for all instruments in a system to "go to" a particular song that is stored in a sequencer. While the song is playing back, system common messages tick off the measures as they go by, which is helpful if you want to edit the song, identify problem spots, etc.

2. *System real-time* messages, just as their name implies, are MIDI's timekeepers. That is, they take care of all the basic "clocking" functions that hold a MIDI sequencer system in sync. MIDI clock data is based on a twenty-four-pulse-per-quarter-note scheme. In a process called interleaving, MIDI clock bits are dropped into the data stream at regular intervals, providing a timing guide which is transmitted over all channels. Time waits for neither man nor machine, which is why MIDI allows all these real-time messages to interrupt the data stream whenever they need to. System real-time messages are also what make it possible to hit the "Start", "Stop" and "Reset" controls on your sequencer and have all the instruments respond accordingly.

3. *System exclusive* messages are a kind of window which opens out onto the future of MIDI. As people find new applications for MIDI (Curing cancer? Splitting the atom?), system exclusive is likely to be the means by which they implement these applications. The original impetus behind system exclusive was to let manufacturers of several MIDI instruments develop "custom" messages that they could pass among their instruments without messing up the normal flow of MIDI. To achieve this, each manufacturer of MIDI products is assigned an identification code number which is included in the status byte that starts off a system exclusive message.

But system exclusive data is not the sole property of the manufacturer who holds a particular ID number. The MIDI Manufacturers' Association (the main MIDI organization here in the States) strongly urges its members to publish the details of their system exclusive implementations. This is what makes it possible to have voicing and patch librarian software, for example, such as the DX-Pro, CZ-Rider, etc. These programs use system exclusive to get inside synths like the DX7 or CZ-101 and simplify programming for the end user.

One of the neatest new applications for system exclusive is its use as a medium for transferring and storing digital samples from the many MIDI sampling devices that are starting to come on the market. The technical board of the MMA is now at work on a standard format for dumping samples. A provisional version of this format has already appeared in the September '85 Bulletin of the IMA (which functions as *the* MIDI user's group, and, as such, the information bureau for the MMA).

Essentially, the dumping of samples involves a fairly elaborate "header", or series of status bytes, in which the manufacturer's system exclusive ID byte is followed by bytes identifying the sampling rate and sampling frequency of the system, the length of the sample and other vital pieces of information. All this is a preamble to the sample data itself. MIDI system designer/manufacturer and MMA chairman Jim Cooper elaborates:

"The format can handle anywhere from eight to twenty-eight bits of quantization. The header also spells out the sampling rate in nanoseconds, so just about any conceivable rate can be accommodated. The header also provides information as to whether there's a loop point present. If you're dumping from an Emulator II, for example, you can specify what the loop points are for any given sound at any given point in time. On the whole, it looks like a very thorough and useful format."

By now it should be clear that, although there are technically just four basic types of MIDI messages (channel messages and the three categories of system messages), there are virtually no limits to the kinds of information MIDI can be used to convey.

Nightlife Among the MIDI Modes.

Now that you know how MIDI data is configured, let's look at how it's transmitted from one instrument to another. Think of an instrument receiving MIDI data as a popular nightclub with a fluctuating door policy. On some evenings, the management's policy is to let *everybody* in. On other nights, things are more exclusive; only a select group of patrons is recognized and admitted. It's the same thing with our MIDI instrument. All the data that's in the cable presents itself at the MIDI In port, but the instrument can react to this mob in a number of different ways. It can recognize all sixteen channels' worth of data. (MIDI has a name for this door policy; it's called Omni.) Or it can limit its response to certain channels only. How can it tell which is the elite data? Easy: the dress code. The "right kind" of data will be wearing the correct channel number on its channel message status byte.

Now we'll push the analogy one step further. Not only can a nightclub choose which customers get in the door, it can also choose how they'll be treated once they're in. The club can throw open all of its facilities or decide to open up just one room. It's the same thing with a MIDI synth. It can make all of its voices available to incoming MIDI data (assuming it's a polyphonic machine). Or it can open up just one voice and operate monophonically. And if it's one of those chic new multitimbral *boîtes*, it can let in several different channels of data and send each one off to a different group of voices, making sure there's no intermingling among different classes of data.

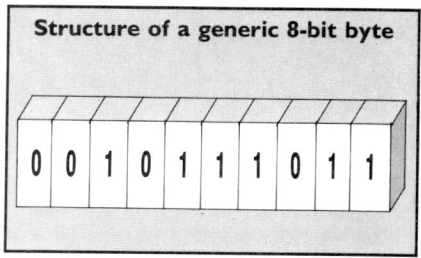

Structure of a generic 8-bit byte

0 0 1 0 1 1 1 0 1 1

Putting all of these different options together, the MIDI Spec identifies four basic modes for receiving data:

Mode 1: *Omni On/Poly*. Probably the most "straightforward" MIDI mode. The receiving instrument responds to messages transmitted on all sixteen channels. Note messages are polyphonically assigned to all the instruments' voices. This mode is often referred to simply as the "Omni Mode."

Mode 2: *Omni On/Mono*. As in mode 1, the receiving instrument responds to messages on all channels. The difference is that all incoming note messages are assigned to just one voice. This mode is used to get a polyphonic instrument to play monophonically. It is one of two modes commonly called "Mono Mode" (see below); so make sure you get your terms straight if you're buying a piece of gear or hooking up with another MIDI musician.

Mode 3: *Omni Off/Poly*. The receiving instrument only responds to messages coming in on one designated channel; but note messages are assigned polyphonically. Generally known as the "Poly Mode," this is one of the most important modes within MIDI. Mode 3 is the one you use when you want a central controller, such as a sequencer, to send out different, but synchronized polyphonic musical passages to different MIDI instruments.

Mode 4: *Omni Off/Mono*. This is the "other Mono Mode." It's an important one too. Thanks to Mode 4, a single multitimbral instrument (such as an Oberheim Matrix-12 or Sequential Six-Trak) can be used to play a number of different musical lines. As we mentioned earlier, a multitimbral system can be programmed to receive several different channels of MIDI information and assign each channel to one or more of its voices. So suppose you had an eight-voice multitimbral synth. You could have a monophonic bass part coming in on one channel and a monophonic melody line coming in on another. Using one voice per channel to build chords, other channels could be used to bring in two three-voice accompaniment parts, or one six-voice accompaniment, or any other combination you wanted.

Channels Vs. Tracks.

Now we come to another great area of MIDI mystification. The sixteen MIDI *channels* are one thing and the number of *tracks* on a MIDI sequencer are something else entirely. Channels exist within the MIDI protocol itself as a way of organizing MIDI data. All MIDI data travels down the same wire, which means that the channels exist solely as numbers within the channel message status byte. It isn't as though there were sixteen separate wires or anything like that.

Tracks, on the other hand, are not a part of the MIDI protocol itself. What they are is a feature included in MIDI sequencers enabling the user to organize his musical data in roughly the same way he would organize his music on a multitrack tape machine. A quick look at today's MIDI sequencer market will underscore the difference between channels and tracks. Although there are just sixteen MIDI channels, there are several thirty-two-track and even sixty-four-track sequencers out there. And by the same token, even if you have a simple one- or two-track MIDI sequencer like a Yamaha QX7, you can still operate on all sixteen MIDI channels. The ability to merge tracks on a MIDI sequencer is what makes these wonders possible. And once again, the key to it all is that simple-but-effective concept of interleaving different types of bytes in a stream of MIDI data. Jeff Rona explains:

"Say you're merging two tracks down to one, and let's assume that each track is on a different MIDI channel. Well, there's a status byte which specifies which MIDI channel each data byte is associated with. And because of this, you can interleave MIDI data with no problem. The only thing that changes is that you may need to add status bytes when you have data interleaving from two tracks down to one. This way, the new, merged track always remembers which data comes from channel one, which from channel two, etc., and where it's all going."

The Notorious Time Lag.

This brings us to another tricky bit. Apart from the inner workings of the 1.0 protocol itself, MIDI time lags are probably the greatest source of heated conversation, mass confusion and wrinkled brows among MIDI users. It all stems from the fact that MIDI, as we've mentioned several times already, is a serial interface. It operates at a rate of 31.25 Kbaud, which means that it takes about 320 microseconds to transmit one byte of MIDI data in the interface's "single file" fashion.

Now here's where the trouble begins. When the data stream for a given message starts getting too complex (i.e., when it contains a lot of bytes), a bottleneck develops. To return to our nightclub analogy, this is what happens on a busy night. They're only letting 'em in one at a time, so there's an annoying wait while everybody lines up to get in. But there's more at stake here than a boring time for our little club-going MIDI bit. There is more data than the receiving instrument can process in order to play the notes right on time. Needless to say, this can wreak havoc in a programmed performance. For this reason, some observers have suggested that MIDI would have been better off as a parallel interface, in which the data travels along separate, parallel lines, thereby speeding up the rate of transmission. "Why not open up a few more doors to the club?" these people argue.

As one of the original movers behind the MIDI 1.0 Specification, Dave Smith of Sequential has answered more than his share of questions about MIDI time lag problems. Smith was instrumental in initiating the "MIDI Talks" between Yamaha, Roland, Korg, Kawai and Sequential. With a little imagination, it's pretty easy to visualize the diplomatic finesse required to get five top manufacturers—competitors no less—to reach a consensus on something as complex and detailed as MIDI. The 1.0 Specification represented some compromises, Smith readily admits. But, he goes on to insist, the reasons for making it a serial interface were quite sound. Many people assume that the serial format was adopted to help keep cabling between instruments simple and inexpensive. But that, Smith exlains, was only part of the story.

"For me," he says, "electrical isolation was just as important as the cost factor and simplicity of the connector. If we had gone parallel, electrical isolation would have become very difficult. Everyone knows how bad ground loop problems are, even without MIDI. Start adding additional connections between instruments—especially digital connections as opposed to audio connections—and the problem is compounded. It would have been almost impossible to keep out ground loops if MIDI had been a parallel interface."

Besides, all the MIDI experts we spoke with agreed that most MIDI time lag problems do not stem from MIDI itself, but from the types of software and microprocessors (commonly Z80s and 6809s) used in MIDI instruments. Because they have to take care of internal control functions *and* process incoming MIDI data, they often can't process the data as fast as MIDI can transmit it.

"It only takes a millisecond to send out a MIDI command," Jim Cooper observes. "But on a DX7, for example, it takes roughly seven milliseconds before notes start sounding."

What's more, MIDI is designed to make the most of its 31.25 Kbaud rate. In transmitting a series of note commands, for example, it will automatically kick into something called running status, which eliminates unnecessary status bytes. Result: what's referred to as a faster thru-put rate.

"Once you've specified 'this is a note on, which happens on Channel 1,'" elaborates Jeff Rona, "then you don't need to send any more status bytes until you're sending something other than a note on. Running status, in other words, is implied status. It means, 'Whatever the last status byte was, it holds for these data bytes as well, until otherwise specified.' This gives you a potential thirty percent compression of data. Typically, a note on command is three bytes long. You have a status byte, the pitch value and the velocity. If you're going to follow that uninterruptedly with several more note ons, you can skip the status byte."

For those of you who *still* aren't satisfied that MIDI's serial baud rate is fast enough for you, there are hints abroad that it may double. And the "digital sampling explosion" may just be the factor that makes this new "double standard" a reality.

"The amount of data in a sampler just blows away the amount of data in any other keyboard instrument," Dave Smith comments. "Take the new Prophet 2000 for example, which has about 256,000 twelve-bit words of data. And we're going to have an expander out pretty soon which will double that. That's a whole lot of data to send out when you're only transmitting 31,000 bits per second. You're starting to talk minutes of transfer time. Doubling the MIDI baud rate would be very simple and viable to achieve. It would help immensely in transmitting sample data and cut in half all these time delays people are talking about. Existing hardware could handle the doubling pretty easily. It only requires a few hardware changes to make the instrument select between the double speed and normal speed. In time, maybe even a 4X MIDI rate will begin to make sense."

The Revised Standard Revisited.

We started out by talking about the new addendum to the MIDI 1.0 Specification. It seems like a good place to finish up as well. This detailed new document signals an important coming of age of MIDI. The era of embarrassing incompatibilities between different manufacturers' MIDI products seems to be drawing to a close. Scores of new companies are getting on the MIDI track without any major derailments. In short, things are looking up for MIDI consumers. They have more choices and fewer worries about different pieces of equipment not working together.

Now that MIDI's awkward stage appears to be over, the technical people at the MMA and IMA have been able to go back and clean up some of the housekeeping details of MIDI implementation—how much delay time is allowable when interleaving MIDI clocks with on and off bits, how the "all notes off" command differs in each of the four modes...that sort of thing. According to Jeff Rona, the new addendum to the 1.0 Spec will also formalize a lot of de facto standards that have grown up in implementing MIDI. Here we're talking about things like code numbers for breath controllers, footpedals and other accessories. As more

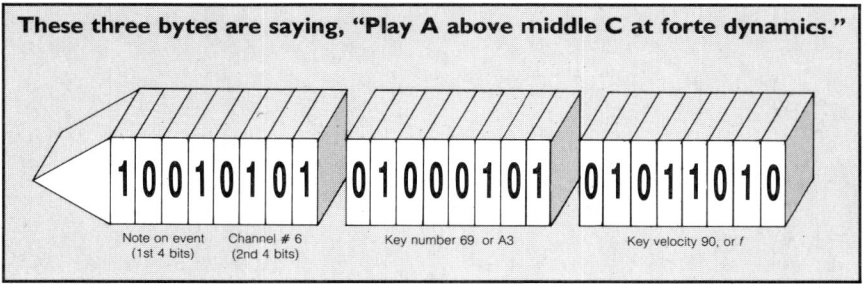

These three bytes are saying, "Play A above middle C at forte dynamics."

`1 0 0 1 0 1 0 1` `0 1 0 0 0 1 0 1` `0 1 0 1 1 0 1 0`

Note on event Channel # 6 Key number 69 or A3 Key velocity 90, or *f*
(1st 4 bits) (2nd 4 bits)

and more sophisticated pitch-to-MIDI conversion devices make it possible to use any traditional instrument as a MIDI controller, more official code number assignments are likely in the future.

MIDI musicians everywhere can benefit more directly from Part Three of the new MIDI document. It contains a standard format and detailed instructions for manufacturers to use in creating implementation charts for their MIDI products. If you're buying a new device for your existing MIDI setup, this should make it easier than ever to gauge how well different products will match up with what you've got already. Want to know if that new drum pad will accept MIDI clock data from your sequencer? Wondering whether that new keyboard can receive all the velocity data your

Roland MKB-1000 sends out? All you have to do is A/B the MIDI implementation charts for each instrument.

Apart from the implementation charts, a good working knowledge of the MIDI protocol itself is your best weapon against unsuccessful hookups. When Box A doesn't seem to respond to Box B, you can start asking the right kind of questions. "Can Box B receive in the Omni Off/Mono Mode?" "Am I transmitting and receiving on the same channel?" If you've read this far, you should already have a pretty good idea of what kinds of questions to ask. And the next time someone hands you a line about MIDIing to Mars by 1995, don't buy unless he can tell you how many status bytes it takes to achieve escape velocity.

Of Plugs & Bugs.

A Harrowing and Hard-Boiled Look at How Everyman Found True MIDI Happiness.
By Jock Baird.

If you've read this far into this special MIDI issue, you're probably beginning to develop a curious light in your eyes, accompanied by serious twitching in fingers anxious to get on some of these setups. Well, let's throw a bit of cold water on all this techno-optimism right now, because I'm going to tell you what no one else in this issue will dare: This MIDI stuff is *hard*! And I ought to know—I just finished setting up a MIDI studio in my basement, and anyone who tells you it's as simple as plugging in an electric guitar is either an M.I.T. post-grad or running for president.

For many novices like myself, the nuts & bolts details of hooking MIDI gear together have been shrouded in generalities. How *does* it all plug together, how does it work, what buttons do you push, what are the positives and negatives, and what kind of money are we talking here? It was clearly time to do some heavy hands-on investigation, and what follows is one man's epic story of trial, tribulation and eventual triumph. When you get started hooking up your own MIDI gear, you'll solve different problems on other equipment, but fundamentally you'll go through the same process.

Getting to Know You.

I started with the basics: A synth and a drum machine, both with MIDI INs and OUTS, both from Sequential Circuits. (Sequential's Dave Smith is widely—and justifiably—credited with being a major force in establishing the MIDI standard, so I figured I was on safe ground.) I'll spare you descriptions of the kinds of awful patterns we guitarists write on drum machines, or the "bitch-in-C" keyboard heroics we manage, but they did teach me a bit about what the pair were capable of.

The drum box was called the Tom (Model 420), and in addition to good cymbal sounds, it had tunability and a plug-in ROM cartridge with seven more Latin percussion or electronic drum samples—rare in an $800 kit. It also had a defective power supply cord, until I had a TV shop test it. They told me the short was in the molded DIN plug into the Tom (with, natch, a difficult-to-find pin pattern). Not wanting to drive an hour each way (during working hours) to buy a new one, I jury-rigged a severe bend with duct tape that (most times) kept the Tom on and pumping.

Its session-mate was called the Multi-Trak, a $1,500 analog job with a small on-board sequencer. This could record six different voices in as many as six different presets, and with 1,600 notes of memory I could do a lot of fiddling. It had only one oscillator per voice, so it lacked some punch, but by doubling, tripling, stacking and splitting those six voices, it could make a lot of music. Like its noble ancestor, the Prophet 5, the Multi-Trak's sounds were definitely analog traditional (including the Keith Emerson patch from "Lucky Man"). But best of all, it had a smooth, velocity-sensitive keyboard (yup, with aftertouch), and therefore became our designated MIDI controller.

Meanwhile, down in the depths of my basement, the foil-faced insulation, new wiring and recycled rugs were in place, and I dusted off four old three-way kick-ass stereo speakers I had built as kits from a small Seattle company called Speakerlab ($240 apiece). I'm a bit of a bear on three-way speakers, ones that have a woofer, tweeter and midrange drivers. The middle frequencies of all that synth/sampling gear just get too jumbled together in a two-way, to say nothing of yer bread-and-butter guitar or bass amp. And I really wanted that *whump* of the kick drum to go through me.

Next I banged together a rough 19-inch rack out of scrap lumber and loaded on a Harman/Kardon power amp, an old Radio Shack preamp unit, a couple of simple Biamp reverbs and topped it off with a 6-in/2-out Heathkit mixer, aided and abetted by a Yamaha Portastudio MM10 which let me pan four mono inputs. As you could guess, my mixing and signal processing was Mickey Mouse, but the synths and samples took up most of the slack. I was ready to begin the MIDI Odyssey.

First MIDI Connections.

Purchasing a MIDI cable at my local dealer ($17.95 for an 18-footer? Say, this stuff ain't cheap), I got ready to MIDI the two Sequential sisters together and see what happened. I hooked both audio outs to my monitor system (remember, MIDI carries no audio itself—you always have to plug a conventional phone jack in) and connected one end of the 5-pronged DIN cord into the MIDI OUT jack of the Tom, and the other into the MIDI IN of the Multi-Trak. Then, as the manual suggested, I turned off the internal metronome of the sequencer and punched in a drum pattern. For the purposes of reader interest, I was ready to carefully observe and then wax eloquent on the Significance Of It All. Instead, hitting the Tom's start button nearly made me fall out of my chair. Out of the speakers came the most startling, dissonant, provocative cacophony I'd ever heard. A random series of organ notes was soloing frenetically over a terse descending chord figure, perfectly synched to the drum pattern I'd punched in. At least I knew where *that* had come from—what was the rest? Was it a sequence? It didn't seem to be repeating, and I hadn't recorded anything like this....

Unbeknownst to me, however, my four-year-old daughter and her friend had. Cheerfully letting them doodle on the keyboard, I never thought they'd be able to accidentally record their own sequence, but that's what they'd done. What blew me away was the MIDI connection synching these utterly random pitches to a tempo, and then adding in new pitches of its own, triggered by the sixteenth-note high-hat beats and whatever else was sounding. Starting the sequencer with no external sync revealed just how chaotic it was. But synched and augmented with MIDI—my God, it was almost music!

Trying the other three sequences, I found myself on safer ground. At least they were in a key and had a tempo. The drums locked right in to the bass and chord patterns and made my keyboard playing seem almost non-wimpy. After a bit, I stopped the sequen-

cer, only to discover that the drum pattern was also softly triggering notes on the Multi-Trak, at least on certain presets. This gave an enhanced tonality to my rhythm patterns I rather liked at first, especially when I used some of the percussive sounds like African Log or Syn Tom. (I noticed also that whatever pattern number I punched on the Tom appeared on the Multi-Trak—although pattern 25 had no useful relation to preset 25.) But after the novelty had worn off a bit, I began to feel those little tonalities were too gimmicky. Still, the MIDI sync had really heated up the onboard sequencer. What would it do going the other direction?

I reversed the connection, plugging the MIDI OUT of the Multi-Trak into the MIDI IN of the Tom, and a pleasant surprise awaited me (well, it wasn't *that* surprising—I read about it in the Tom's MIDI Manual first). The lower half of the Multi-Trak's keyboard now triggered the drum sounds as well as the synth sounds. By turning down the Multi-Trak's audio output, I could get just drums. Moreover, instead of only eight working buttons at a time on the Tom panel, I now had separate keys for all fifteen Tom sounds, with some of them doubled for easy rolls or high-hat patterns, and they could write patterns for the internal memory. But more compelling was the Tom's new-found velocity sensitivity. Each drum voice in the Tom can be set to one of seven volume levels internally, but if you set the snare to volume 5, it stays there until you change it again. MIDI'd to the Multi-Trak, however, that snare could be any one of the seven volume levels depending on how hard I hit the keyboard. This gave the Tom major-league humanity and spontaneity. From that time on, I never used the instrument buttons on the Tom front panel, and my drum parts got a lot better. MIDI had definitely made the two units greater than the sum of their parts.

The Longest Upgrade.

My experiments had given me some insight into what MIDI could do, but what was required was a device to digitally record all this, a centerpiece. Thus I began the search for a computer. I wasn't starting from scratch in this department, for in the course of my job I'd inherited a 256K IBM-XT, a PC with a hard disk; but there were two reasons why this was not the free ride it seemed to be. Number one was that it was black and white, and needed a $250 color graphics card to work for music, and might require a color monitor as well—IBMs don't run on regular TVs like Commodores do. Number two, and more seriously, comparatively little music software is written for the PC as compared to the C-64 or Apple (IBM is a big-business-oriented computer and musicians are said to be loath to identify with conglomerates like Big Blue). So I went out and did some cost comparisons, discovering that for the same $600 it would cost to upgrade the PC I could buy a complete Commodore C-64, monitor and disk drive (the cost of a new Apple or Mac was too prohibitive to be a legit option). For many days I agonized over the choice, when it suddenly hit me: How could I trade my big 80-character wide screen, four times the memory, and that classy IBM type, for a computer I'd buy from a toy store? I resolved to stick with Big Blue, although I was buying into a higher degree of difficulty.

How difficult I would soon discover, but my spirits soared when Roland offered to assist in the writing of this article by loaning me a new copy of Kentyn Reynolds' fabulous transcribing and recording Music Processing System, or MPS. Listing for $500, it comes in a large turquoise shrink-wrap package that resembles a huge book. Roland also provided two more essentials, the MPU-401, the first computer interface to appear on the market nearly two years ago, and a circuit board called the MIF-I PC that plugs into the inside of my computer, which the MPU-401 in turn plugs into. You mean I have to open up my $2,000 computer and put in new electronics? Yup. Not just the MIF, but my new Quadram color card as well.

Here I have to confess I was feeling

pretty bullish about things. My attitude could essentially be described as "Hey, I'm a reasonably smart person; if I read the manual it'll be easy." Carefully I removed the five screws on the back and pulled the cover off. To the left rear of the flat box, sure enough were the circuit boards, all lying on their sides. With studied precision I snapped in the two slides, then slid in the Quadram, right next to the black and white board. Hmmm, the board's little gold connectors were not going down in the holes. How hard should I push? What if I snapped the board in half? I pushed a little harder to no avail, then regrouped. Say, why not make the hold-down screw at the top do the work? (It works on cars.) I tightened it down and the board dropped in. The MIF was similarly dispatched in short order. Reassembling the computer, I patted myself on the back. Easy stuff this.

The Quadram manual specifically said their board would work with the monochrome board in my IBM, so I'd left it in. My black and white monitor got no signal when I plugged it into the jack on the new color card, but worked fine off its old board, so I proceeded, cabling the MPU-401 to the back of the computer with the RS-232 computer plug that came with the MIF, and then ran MIDI cords from the Tom and the Multi-Trak to the MPU-401. Now came the moment to boot the program—oh, sorry, to put the MPS diskette into the disk drive and start up the program. I typed in RUN, which the manual told me to do. The words "echo off" flashed, then "initialize MPU-401." Then nothing. Messages, messages...I muttered, looking through the appendix. No, not even in the MPU-401 manual.

Then I saw the apparent reason: "You

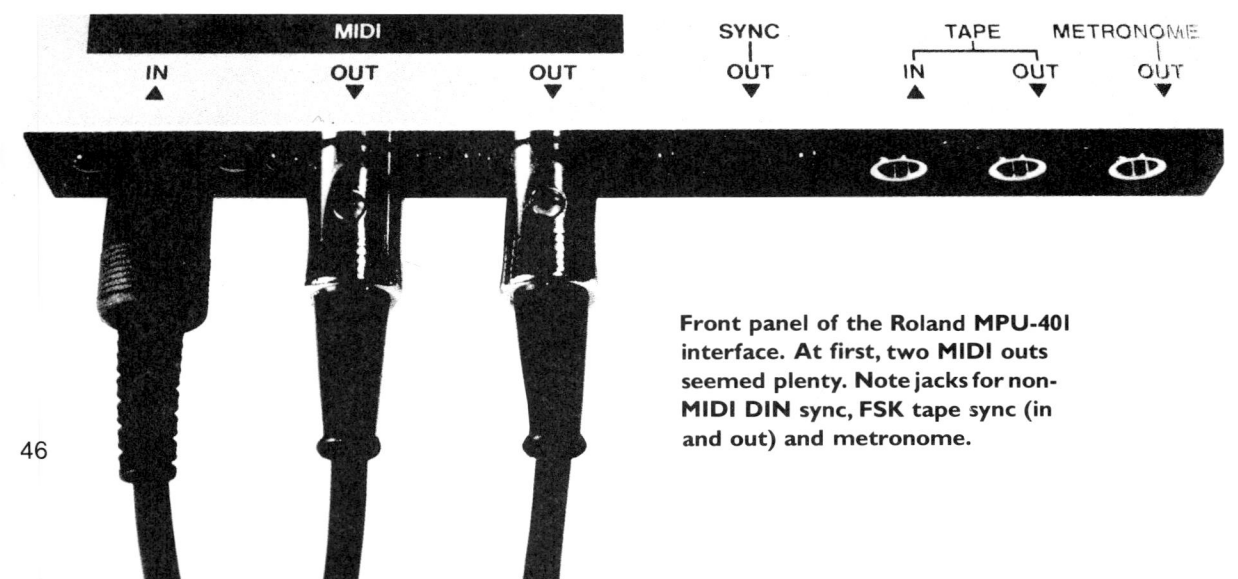

Front panel of the Roland MPU-40I interface. At first, two MIDI outs seemed plenty. Note jacks for non-MIDI DIN sync, FSK tape sync (in and out) and metronome.

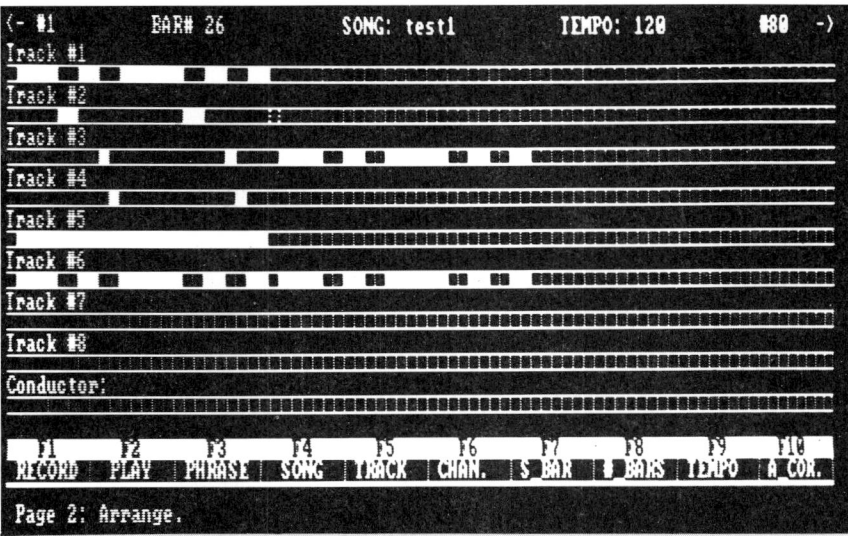

Display for MPS' Score mode; note filled bars at top and menu boxes at bottom.

cannot run MPS from the disk which comes with this package," the MPS manual said, going on to describe a software locking program used to prevent unauthorized copying. "To make a run-time disk, you must use the enclosed disk to install MPS onto a different floppy or hard disk." That was it! Well no wonder. I then began an attempt to follow the copy procedure. There was only one copy allowed, and that gave small room for error. I made mine when I followed MPS' directions to copy what's known in IBMese as my Disk Operating System, or DOS, onto a new floppy disk. Actually they said the DOS *system* files, which I later learned means just a few significant files, but I copied the whole DOS disk, leaving no room for the MPS program. The Sunday afternoon begun in bright optimism degenerated into a grim retracing of the same pages in the manual, trying to reconcile apparently conflicting directions, always ending with the same galling "initialize MPU-401." I was stuck, I was pissed, I felt completely impotent. At the end of launch day, my MIDI spaceship was stranded on the pad.

The next day I called Roland's help line and a nice fellow named Scott Wilkinson soothed my frazzled nerves. In fact, the MPS disk *would* boot just the way I'd done it, and though he wasn't sure how to solve it, my problem was that the color card was not functioning. He suggested just putting the Quadram into the black and white slot. I pulled the top off the IBM and did just that, but the monitor remained dark and, more ominously, there was no activity in the main computer. Then, after going through the IBM Guide to Operations, I came upon a section which showed different switch setups, and also a previously unnoticed passage from the Quadram manual that stated "certain system board switches must be set." I finally located these switches, which, I kid you not, were packed eight-wide on a pad the size of a postage stamp. Good God, what do they want from me now, microsurgery?

I reconfigured the switches for color, and tried the black and white monitor on the color output. Nothing, but at least something was working inside the big box. I installed the black and white card in a new slot, plugged in the black and white and fired it up again (by this time, I was powering up with the cover off, throwing caution to the winds). Finally, despite what I had been told, I was left with one last choice: Pull out the monochrome and borrow a color monitor. A friend who was still awake had one and I drove across town to pick it up with a cold determination. It was very late when I got home, and I had told myself to wait until morning to try it, mostly to spare myself further agony. But I had to know. I plugged it in and turned on the PC. The screen lit up and the prompt appeared. Trembling, I inserted the MPS disk and typed RUN for the fortieth time. The program whirred for a few seconds, and then "Roland presents MPS" shot on the screen with a menu at the bottom. A Mark Gastineau sack dance ensued—I was in! Victory at last!

47

Menu Madness.

The one thing all computer programs share is a system of menus. A menu in a computer does what it does in a restaurant: Gives you the digital dishes the chef has been trained to prepare. Some software menus, like the pfs Write I'm using now, fit on a page or two, which you can get to any time just by hitting the Escape key. This won't hurt anything I'm typing—that stays in a separate buffer in the memory that I can get back to off the menu page. A complex program like MPS, though, does too many things to fit on one page, so it uses a kind of branch system. You start at a ground-level trunk called the System page. From there you have the choice of entering three so-called modes: A recording/arranging one, SONG (which we'll spend most of our time in), a transcription/notation one, SCORE (which we'll dabble in), and a Print one (which needs 64K more memory that I've got. Sorry, no tickee, no laundee.) Within each mode there are separate pages of menu options, as assigned to the Function keys on the left side of the keyboard. Hoo boy, I can tell I'm losing you.

Let's look at it this way. The first thing you'll see upon booting the program is the System page, which is also Page 1 in any mode. Now, look at the bottom of the screen. MPS, like Basic, uses a row of boxes to tell you what its ten function keys are set up to do at any given moment—for instance, I don't have to remember that Function key 9 is the one that lets me type in a new tempo; the F9 box says TEMPO. This is the way most computer programs do business. If it's a good one, it will do more than give you choices—it'll ask you questions like "Are you *sure* you want to erase your only copy of this file?" Or "Don't turn on the external clock, dummy!"

So, now that we've got the system page up, let's hit F2. "Song Mode?" double checks MPS. Yes, I say by hitting return. Bingo. The screen changes to nine rows of eighty boxes (eighty measures of eight tracks plus a conductor for beat and tempo changes). We can see lots more than eighty bars simply by moving the cursor off the screen to the right. Again at the bottom, there's a new set of menu commands. This is called Page 2, Arrange, my home base for recording operations. By hitting the Page Up and Page Down keys, I can

Workhorse function keys on IBM-PC

see both the original system menu (in case I want to go to the other mode or exit) and another menu called Page 3, MIDI, which handles more detailed control tasks. I took a bit of time just paging through the menus, aided by my trusty Escape key: No matter how convoluted an operation I attempt in these subfunctions, like muting tracks, assigning channels or telling MPS when to punch in, I can always throw up my hands and hit Escape, bringing me back to Page 2 or 3. This is really just computer navigation, and an hour spent fiddling with the six menus (there are two other pages in SCORE, and one in PRINT) left me confident and ready to try to record something.

I am now looking at Page 2, Arrange. The menu reminders say F1 is Record. F2 is Play. That's good enough for me, I said, and hit F1. A message told me I was set up to record and to hit the space bar when ready. Why the space bar? It's the biggest key on the keyboard, and in the heat of recording, you don't want to be looking for some obscure little key. I hit the bar and heard a quiet metronome click coming out of the MPU-401, two musical tones, one higher than the other so the beat won't turn around in your mind. Unfortunately I could barely hear this and botched the timing of my first track. The space bar was the Stop button as well as the start (not unlike your neighborhood drum box), and I hit it. There was a brief pause, and then the message said, perhaps a bit too brightly, "Finished! Select F1, F2, F3 or Insert."

Definitely time to record again! F1, please. But first, I connected a guitar cord out of the metronome plug of the MPU-401 and sure enough I was able to get that beep tone into the monitor system. After one more pass of the space bar and F2 (Play), I got a very marginal piano part down. This meant I had recorded it into what MPS calls its Phrase buffer. I hit F2 for a playback, and damn if it didn't play back! There's something really magical about your first playback, when the computer actually shows you it's a perfectly decent real-time recorder. No moving reels, just the little measure counter changing, and all this sound coming out. Unbelievable! So now I had what MPS calls a Phrase. I could save it by itself on a disk, or use the insert key to insert it into the top row of boxes, track one. I chose the latter, moving the cursor to the left of the row and hitting Insert. "Insert phrase starting from bar #1? Y/N" the eager beaver computer asked. I hit Y. The empty boxes on the top row filled

The author's studio (pre-Mirage)

solid with my deathless part, and I had begun creating a Song.

Hitting F1 (Record) again gave me my old track and the metronome, so I put down a bass line using the same piano sound. I played it back, hitting the F2 (Play) key, but all I got was the bass part alone. Not what I wanted to hear, so I inserted the second line into the song, hit F2, and both parts came back. In this way, I came to know the four keys (F1, F2, Insert and Space) that would do the bulk of my work for me. In virtually no time, they became second nature to me, as did other essentials like the Auto Correct buttons.

Stuck In Omniland.

At this point, a friend came over with his Korg Poly 800 and we began experimenting. Setting both the Multi-Trak and the Tom to channel 10, and turning down the volume of the keyboard, I was again able to trigger drum sounds (the configuration of MIDI cables into the MPU-401 had the same effect as the direct plug-in I'd done before, but this time the performance was recorded). We did two tracks of rhythm and played them back together. These had the advantage of being completely in real time—no repeats at all. Combined with the velocity sensitivity, the pair of drum parts were a splendid foundation for a song. We were rolling now!

Or so we thought. What followed was two hours of extreme frustration. As soon as we tried to get the Korg into the system, unhooking the Multi-Trak since there were only two outputs from the MPU-401, we discovered to our horror that everything was playing everything. The drum parts, in addition to sounding on the Tom, also sounded the Poly 800's keys. When we killed the playback, the drums would still double the Korg's notes. What was clear was that we were stuck in Omniland, a zone where everything was playing everything. Unfurling several manuals (and recalling Alan di Perna's Protocol article), we vainly attempted to sort everything out. On two occasions I located what I was convinced was the problem: I reassigned the MPS channels at the computer—no go. Then I discovered in an appendix of the Tom manual how to take the drums out of this remote keyboard control mode, but this affected the MIDI signal from the MPS as well, so there was no drum playback at all even as the Poly 800 continued to play the drum parts with a bass preset. By the end of a frustrating evening, unable to solve the unison problem, we contented ourselves with MIDIing the synths together and trying sound mixes, an impressive demonstration of another MIDI capability, but a poor second to an evening of eight-track recording.

What had gone wrong? Actually a convergence of three factors, which had made it extremely difficult to troubleshoot. Number one was my habit of turning off the Multi-Trak to silence the odd moans that stray MIDI data were causing. Most of the time, the all-important channel and mode settings were unchanged, but once or twice the default setting of omni mode (Mode 1) had reappeared and I hadn't checked it. Number two was caused by a too-rapid reading of the MPS manual: The track and mode a part was recorded on was actually part of the playback data. When I thought I had discovered how to reassign the channels, the display *said* I was in a new channel, but in fact I had not pushed the right function key first, so I was still on the old one. Once I read the right section of the manual the next day, my mistake was quickly apparent and I felt a little sheepish.

The third problem, and core culprit: The Poly 800 had been bought eighteen months ago, back in the dark ages of MIDI, and it was stuck permanently in omni! I found out later from Korg that only earlier Poly 800s have this defect, and they offer a free retrofit to correct this. But hindsight makes experts of us all: That night, MIDI was again a dream deferred.

Another problem had reared its head that night: While set up to record drums, I would hit F1 and then the space bar and the keyboard would trigger diddly-squat. I would continually go back to the main menu, turn off the synth, and it would trigger the drum sounds again, up until I hit that space bar after F1 (Record). Repetition brought its own aggravation—WHY won't it work??!! Why is this happening to *me*? Another call to software central brought the suggestion that I hit the Reset MPU-401 function button on the MIDI page, a practice that would also banish my banshees. That seemed to do the trick, but then it began again.

Finally, almost in desperation, I thought of that old power cord problem on the Tom. A MIDI hookup like this one is really a chain, and one weak link like that defective plug could bring it down.

In any case, it made it difficult to trouble-shoot, since it was an on-again/off-again problem, So I bit the bullet, finally drove the two hours during working hours ("Me? No I was here—I was just using Brad's office"), bought the new DIN plug, and survived a wild and wooly soldering experience. The new plug worked! That was a kind of watershed. Although the problem of the disengaging keyboard would return, it never shut down the studio again. Moral: those little Rube Goldberg jobs you've been doing for years with your guitar cords won't cut it in the MIDI era. The voltages are just too sensitive now.

Moral number two: A little manual reading doesn't hurt. I confess that my curiosity about MPS had gotten ahead of my homework, especially since it had seemed pretty straightforward at first. And there were so many manuals...I had also been fudging the Omni-Poly situation. It was time to get—and keep—my channels sorted out. Once I checked that both Multi-Track and Tom were safely in Mode 3 (Omni off, Polyphonic), I could pick some channels. I put the drums on channel ten (a Roland demo disk assignment I retained) and the synth on channel three. Finally I could record two drum parts on my first two tracks using the keyboard with the sound turned off, then play it back with the keyboard ready for action. Multi-track city, at last!

Hey, We're Rolling Now, Bob!

My first stop in the new everything's-starting-to-work-like-the-manual-says phase, or Era of Good MIDI Feelings, was the Keyboard Split section of the Multi-Trak manual, because I needed a good bass patch for track three and a decent chordal patch for tracks four and five (remember, all three of these MPS tracks are coming in and going out on MIDI channel 3, because that's what the keyboard was set on when I recorded). Why two tracks for chords? If you, like me, are not a keyboard player, you might be surprised how easy it is to break complex 4-note chord voicings into two passes of two each. Especially because you only have to get it right once. Say what?

Yes, that was something else I was getting the hang of—the Lift function. Recording five tracks of the opening vamp to my test song, I finally got everything right for about ten bars. That was two more than I needed for the vamp (my opening bars were interesting so I left them in, then lifted out my best eight bars of track one and inserted them into the Phrase buffer). Then I positioned the cursor at the beginning of the measure where I wanted to drop in my eight-bar phrase and hit Insert. "Insert Phrase into Track 4 at bar 19? Y/N," the nervous Nellie of a computer asks. Yes, I reply and the next eight squares fill up with notes. A sight of beauty! And the nicest part about MPS' lifting function is that the measure numbers I told it to copy off of track one are still there, so I can quickly lift and insert the next four tracks of my drums, bass, keyboard section. Now I began to see the real possibilities of cut and paste, especially since I could save anything and everything to that Big Blue disk drive and pull it out later. Meanwhile, though, I hungered for more instruments!

More Keyboards, More Expanders.

Enter another MIDI owner and his Casio CZ-101 synth and Roland TR-707 drumbox—and a rude shock. The MPU-401 had room for a MIDI In from a controller (my Multi-Trak keyboard) and two MIDI OUTs, one to the Tom and one left between the two synths. It was a surprising and distressing education on the value of MIDI THRU plugs in any equipment you buy. (No, the OUT jack didn't send on any channels the synth wasn't set to.) Sure we could mix 'n' match and do overdubbing with a track missing (yuk) but otherwise we were still a synth and a drum machine. Still, MPS did give us an impressive demonstration of its ability to handle patch changes: While recording, my guest executed an absolutely insane sequence of patch changes; the MPS reproduced them on playback, the LEDs dashing back and forth on the panel of the CZ-101.

I immediately got on the phone to buy an inexpensive MIDI through box—the Roland MM-4 was $70 list. But vagaries of the MIDI market made one unavailable on short notice so I had to pay more for a Roland MPU-105. This added on/off switching capabilities (hey, if I wanted 'em off I'd unplug 'em) but now I have to give up another plug for the power supply for the LEDs. Lesson: Order early in your hardware assembly season, 'cause you *will* need a thru-box. Often I wonder about those MIDI stocking problems—"Oh, too bad you have

to spend more in my store"—but at least it's getting better. Last year, MPU-401s were as scarce as Mondale voters.

Meanwhile, at the height of our befuddlement at having four MIDI instruments, eight MIDI tracks, sixteen MIDI channels and only two jacks to plug them into, the cavalry sounded and a Federal Express man delivered a new Ensoniq Multi-Sampler (a Mirage minus keyboard). You mean people don't send *you* $1,400 samplers? Well, I do have to give it back...On it's beautiful back panel was—a MIDI THRU port. Yaaaay!! I plugged the second MPU-401 output into the MIDI IN port of the Mirage. But now I had to get the Ensoniq up. Lord, another manual to decipher—this would be my seventh! Mercifully, the Multi-Sampler had terrific dive-in instructions and quickly I had a slap bass and acoustic piano samples on each half of the keyboard, then plugged the CZ into the THRU port. I then set the Mirage on MIDI channel 4 and the CZ-101 on channel 5.

A light bulb finally clicked on in my mind about MIDI channels. From my Multi-Trak keyboard, with the sound turned down, I could use the channel number knob to be (10) drums, (5) digital CZ-101, (4, lower half of the keyboard) bass *guitar* or (4, top half) piano. And once the MPU-105 came, the Multi-Trak would join the fray. The best of all three sonic worlds at my fingertips...all directly patched to the IBM. In fact, I immediately called up my test song from its home on a floppy disk and changed the Mirage to channel 3. It took over all the split-keyboard parts I'd written on the Multi-Trak. And what a difference! Especially when I tried another MIDI cable out of the OUT port and tapped to the Multi-Trak, which gave a wispy extra dimension to the slightly cold piano sound.

A day or so after I got the Mirage working, however, it started behaving strangely. All at once it would go from a normal piano to this sprongy, awful tremolo. I did my usual turn-it-off-turn-it-on dance but it wasn't buying that for long. It was becoming a major pain when the other side of the keyboard started up. What is this? This made me go through the entire Mirage manual, which did teach me a lot, but which didn't explain my problem. Finally, at the edge of despair I noticed the mod wheel seemed a tad more on than it should. Just moving the wheel sorted out the sprong, but it came back again, only to be driven out by a quick nudge of the wheel. Deciding discretion was the better part of valor, I looked in the Mirage manual for the parameters that disengaged the wheel. End of sprong forever, at least till I want it. This albeit minor problem was the first one I'd solved in the same session it appeared in, and began a new era of confidence for me. There really was some logic to all this, if you looked long enough.

With this inspiration I went ahead and did chorus, vamp, and bridge sections to my test song, some new, some lifted. After completing six tracks (a ringing CZ-101 arpeggio added here and there for dynamics), I listened to the forty or so bars I recorded. Unfortunately, some of the punch-ins were jerky, especially in the bass. I found, though, that by recording another track of touch-ups on the same MIDI channel as the first bass, my new notes would meld in with the others. I was also able to do more real-time tom fills and special effects—using the Tom's electronic drums cartridge and hard blows to the keyboard I succeeded in nearly blowing out all four monitors! Yeah!! Rock 'n' roll! If I fill up all eight tracks, I can merge all three drum or all three Mirage tracks—believe it or not, MPS remembers which notes came from which track if you want to de-combine them later. We're talking music *processing*, baby!

Reflections of the MIDI Life.

I was beginning to notice more general things about MIDI recording sessions. One was that no matter how many people came, only one could play at any one time (a 4-in/1-output box would probably help, but two instruments would have to then share the same phrase—kind of messy). I found the talent of playing to a metronome more important than in regular recording—error correct can only take you so far. This is not to say MPS can't handle freer-metered pieces; if you can make it work out of time, go ahead, but adding drums won't be easy. But for my classical experiment below, it worked fine.

I observed that lack of specific musicianship or technique could almost always be surmounted by a sense of core musicality, patience and concentration. A bad attitude, a show-me attitude, a you-owe-me-attitude was an open invitation to disaster. In the early stages of working with the computer program, for example, it invariably sensed when I was trying to impress studio visitors and would instead embarrass me. And yes, it's hard to run a MIDI studio and be a true party animal—not impossible, I suspect, but harder. One spilled beer and you're in big, big trouble, especially with diskettes around.

I also noticed that most of the time that I or my guest artists were *jamming* on the computer, we would fall into these all-too-familiar Herbie Hancock synth-funk vamps (which only tended to renew my doubts about Herbie's recent output). But when we made MPS do some real work, something specific and organized like arranging a song we knew well, it invariably was more impressive. What am I trying to say here? That a program like this is a *tool*, not a toy. Don't judge MIDI's potential just because we've all gotten sick of all these techno-funk indulgences. It's here to do real jobs for you, not just gratify your more free-associative moments.

I explored two more facets of MPS in the next few days. The first was figuring out how to transpose a phrase in the buffer and drop it into a song, so I could take the same bass line and make it play in different keys. This was not as easy as I thought it was, because the correction in the phrase buffer was a temporary one—I had to modulate a whole track at a time. I solved this by using a separate track for each chord; I'm sure there must have been an easier and more track-efficient way, but I couldn't find it.

The second was more exciting. I asked a pianist I knew to play a few pages of Mozart using the Mirage's acoustic piano sample. After getting several takes, I then had her double the same parts using a bell-like piano sound on the Casio. Once she had done two full parts, I called up strings and cello on the Mirage, a harpsichord on the Multi-Trak and rode the volume slider of the Casio for swells. Instant Mozart in my basement! From this, I feel strongly that MIDI equipment should be given a few hours of classical music every month to warm up its chips and to give it a better reputation....

And I have even more diabolical plans. By saving the parts as long phrases, I can put them into the transcribing option SCORE mode we mentioned earlier. Using the original manuscript (which the program transcribed with surprising accuracy—I did have to use the FORMAT page to set the key signature, get the beaming right, etc.) I can delete everything but selected melody lines and turn them into string or horn parts. I mean, why not learn arranging with some worthy material? After I've done a straightforward orchestration, I may recycle little reprocessed phrases of Mozart. After all, if MIDI could put my kid's random playing in funky time, imagine what it'll do for old Amadeus. I now know also that by putting my Multi-Trak in MIDI mode 4 (omni-off/mono) I can assign a different patch to each of the six voices. Gotta try that soon. I'll also be recording an FSK signal onto my trusty old TEAC 2340 4-track, which will sync all this to tape so I can add guitar and vocals to my test song tracks and still fiddle with them. Otherwise, I'd have to mix 'em down to two stereo tracks. Yes, my obsolete old 4-track just traded one of its tracks for up to eight more, depending on how many Expander modules I can lay my hands on. That's really the rub about this MIDI business. You always want MORE! And I have lots of questions about programming analog sounds. How about a CZ-101 librarian program, or a Yamaha TX7 so I can get in on one of the forty million DX7 voicing programs out there? The more you learn, the more there is to learn.

"So," you observe sardonically, "now you're saying it's *not* that hard. In fact, you're beginning to sound like those other caped crusaders prancing around with big Ms on their chests." Gosh, I don't know what to say. Now that I've been through the crucible of learning this stuff, it *doesn't* seem that hard. But it sure doesn't seem that easy, either. Still, I've reached the point where I can't remember what it was I didn't know, as if most of it really was self-evident at the time. That's probably why most of us who write about MIDI usually won't bore you about the bad power supply, or getting the right peripheral card arrangement, or botching copy procedures, or the horrors of Omniland, or the screaming banshees in the micros, or the still-mysterious disengaging controller, or the warble in the Mirage or any of the other glitches we stumble over, come back to again and again, finally surpass, and then forget with mild embarrassment. We emphasize the glory, as well we should. Because right now I've learned the best way I could've that MIDI really *is* all it's cracked up to be, and if an old hippie like me can figure it out, so can you.

Synchronicity.

How to Get Your Equipment in Sync, from Clock Pulses and FSK to MIDI & SMPTE.
By Craig Anderton.

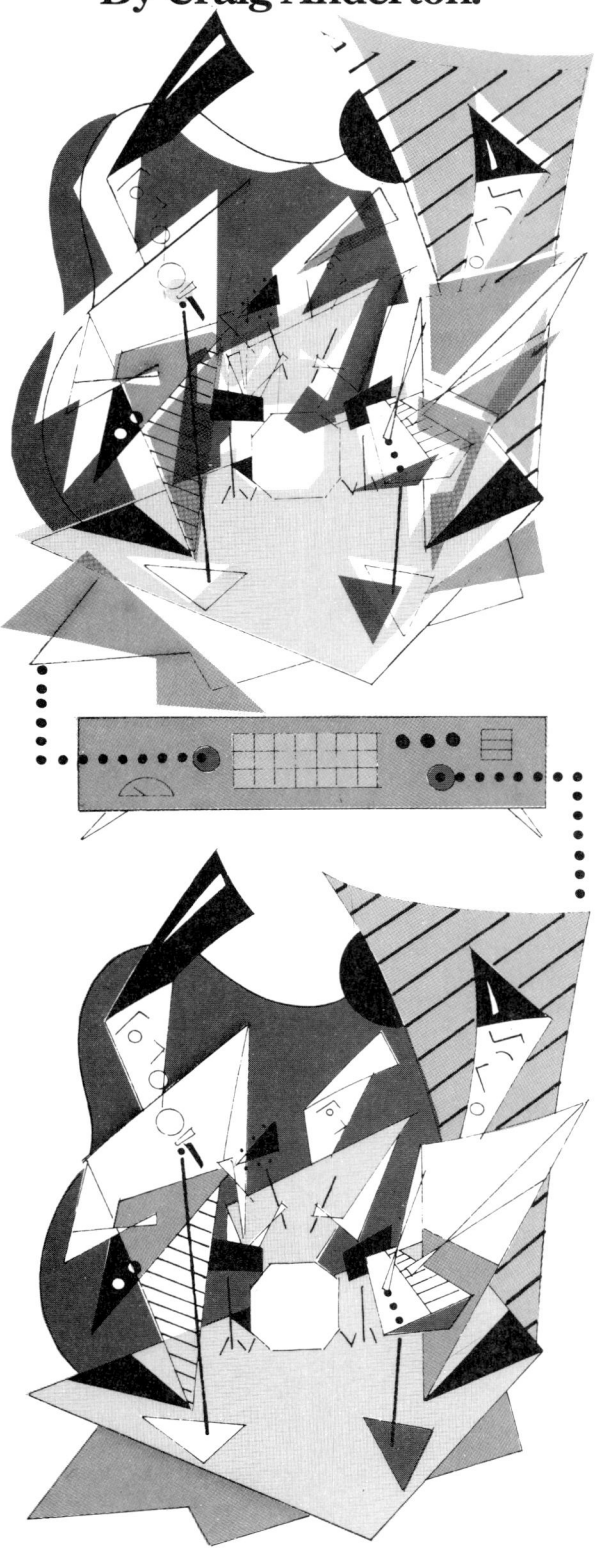

Musical synchronicity has not changed much since people started beating on logs. In fact, it's a lot easier to understand all these mysterious little SMPTE/MIDI/synchronizing boxes if you realize that deep down, all they're really trying to do is emulate human behavior.

With human players, one person (typically a drummer) keeps time and the other players follow that person for their timing cues. The players constantly monitor the drummer to make sure they are properly synchronized, and if the tempo speeds up or slows down a little bit, adjust their speed to compensate.

That's what synchronization is all about: getting every element of a system in sync with the master timekeeper. This article will cover the many possible ways to synchronize, from the earliest clock-pulse based systems on up to SMPTE...and we'll describe some useful applications as well.

Early Synchronization Methods.

The most basic electronic timekeeper, which is still very much in use today, is the *clock*. When turned on (usually at the beginning of a song), the clock emits a steady stream of pulses. Devices such as drums and sequencers count the number of pulses since the clock was first started. Providing that the instruments in the system start counting at the same time and count at the same rate, if the drum machine plays a certain sound at, say, the 345th pulse and the sequencer plays another sound at the 345th pulse, you will hear the two sounds at precisely the same moment.

Each clock pulse is a pulse of energy, like the "tick" or "tock" of a clock. Clock pulses are the electrical equivalent of a pendulum; however, instead of swinging back and forth between two points, a clock pulse swings back and forth between a maximum and minimum voltage (see Fig. 1). This is a very unambiguous type of signal—it's either full on or full off.

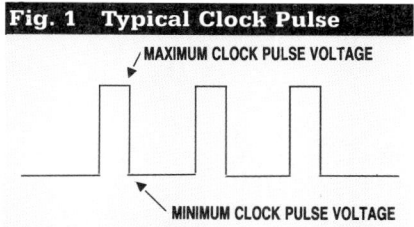

Fig. 1 Typical Clock Pulse

MAXIMUM CLOCK PULSE VOLTAGE

MINIMUM CLOCK PULSE VOLTAGE

The simplest, and least successful, way to synchronize two devices is to set their respective internal clocks for the same tempo and try to start them at the same time. Problem 1: How do you set *exactly* the same tempo for both machines? Even if both devices have tempo readouts, these are not likely to be 100% accurate. The tempo of either device can also drift due to instabilities in electronic components.

Problem 2: The two units must start at *exactly* the same time. If one starts as little as fifteen milliseconds or so behind the other, you will hear an annoying "slapback echo" effect.

The solution to the first problem is to use a *master* clock to provide a common timing reference to all the *slave* devices in the system. Should the master clock drift a little bit, all the slaves following the clock will drift by the same amount, thus maintaining sync. Each slave must have an *external clock input* so that it can accept timing pulses from the master, as well as a means to defeat the slave's internal clock (if present) and select the external clock. The master must have a *clock output* jack to send the timing reference to the slaves.

Now refer to Fig. 2 to see how this all comes together. The master drum machine selects its internal clock; the clock output signal feeds the sequencer and a second drum machine, which are slaved to the master. These latter two devices are switched to accept the external clock signal plugged into their external clock input jacks. However, we still need a way to start all the devices at the same time. For this, each device needs a *start/stop* (also called *run/stop*) input. In most cases we can connect the start/stop inputs together and run them from a single footswitch, thus giving us the option to turn all the devices on simultaneously. As soon as the switch closes, the master starts sending out pulses and the slave devices start counting those pulses.

Great! Now all machines start and stop at the same time and follow the same master timing reference, which means they are in sync with each other. So our problems are solved, right?

Well...not always, which brings us to the "different clock rate" problem.

Different Clock Rates.

Since our tempo reference should be as musically useful as possible, we need to relate the number of pulses to beats and measures. Clock rates are specified in *pulses per quarter note* (ppqn). For example, suppose a sequencer that follows a 24 ppqn standard is set to receive an external clock; the sequencer counts the number of pulses it receives, and each pulse advances the sequence 1/24th of a beat. Therefore, 24 pulses elapse for every beat, and consequently 96 pulses (4 times 24) would elapse during one measure (4 beats) of 4/4 music. Unfortunately, though, different units have different clock rates, and even different hardware to deliver them: there's not only a conventional ¼-inch phone jack version, but a 5-pin DIN plug variety (physically similar to the now-familiar MIDI plug, but there the resemblance ends—avoid plugging one into the other at all costs). Common rates are ¼-inch 24 ppqn (used by E-mu, Moog and Sequential Circuits), DIN 24ppqn (used by Roland), ¼-inch 48 ppqn (favored by Linn), DIN 48 ppqn (Korg's) and 96 ppqn (the Oberheim standard). The Fairlight CMI requires a 384 ppqn clock, and older PPGs 64 ppqn.

If an Oberheim device provides the master clock that feeds a Roland drum machine and Oberheim sequencer, there's a problem; the sequencer will advance 1/96th of a beat every time it counts a clock pulse, but the drum machine (which works on a 24 ppqn standard) will advance 1/24th of a beat for each clock pulse received. Therefore, during the time it takes for the sequencer to play one beat (96 pulses), the drum machine will have played an entire measure. Fortunately, there are a number of adapter boxes from J.L. Cooper Electronics, Garfield Electronics, Korg, Roland, etc. to synchronize machines with different ppqn requirements.

Before going any further, let's explain why these particular numbers were chosen. The reason we want these pulses is to *trigger events*—perhaps a drum beat on a drum machine, or to advance a sequencer to a particular note. Therefore, we have to make sure that wherever we might want to trigger an event, a pulse will be there to provide the trigger. For example, if we only need to trigger an event on every beat, a 1 ppqn system works just fine. But suppose we want to trigger an event on every eighth note. We would then need a 2 ppqn system in order to provide a suitable trigger pulse in between the quarter notes. Every time we increase the number of clock pulses per quarter note, we increase the *resolution*—the

ability of the drum machine or sequencer to program "detailed" rhythms. With a 4 ppqn system events can occur every 16th note, and to trigger 32nd notes, an 8 ppqn system would do since there are eight 32nd notes to every quarter note.

But what about triplets? Unfortunately, 8 ppqn is not divisible by three. After a little bit of research, some companies figured 24 ppqn was the best way to go, as this accommodates up to 32nd notes and 32nd note triplets (Fig. 3). As the figure shows, no matter where you want to trigger a sound—up to 64th note triplets—there will be a corresponding trigger at that point.

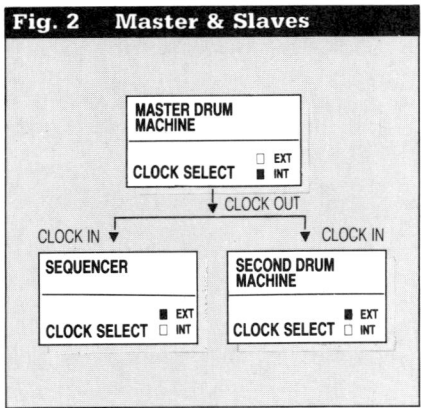

Fig. 2 Master & Slaves

By the way, a clock can do more than just feed drum machines and sequencers; for example, my "Master Synchronizer" derives trigger pulses at regular rates (quarter note, eighth note, sixteenth note, triplets, etc.) from a 24 ppqn clock. These triggers can drive synthesizer arpeggiators, play individual electronic drum sounds, switch effects on and off, etc. The concept that a master timing track can provide information for all kinds of other uses is an important one, as we'll see later when we get into SMPTE time code.

For live music, we have all we need: Upon starting the master, the slaves will count along with the master and stay in sync. But some problems remain. What about synchronizing overdubs to tape? And starting these devices in the *middle* of a song? And what about synchronizing audio to video? Read on...

Synch to Tape.

Suppose you record a rhythm machine track on tape, then several overdubs later decide to overdub another rhythm machine part. If the overdub machine's tempo is *identical* to the tempo of the original part, and if you start the overdubbed part at *exactly* the same time as the previously recorded part, there is a slim possibility that the two will stay in sync long enough to record the overdub. However, if the tape speed varies even a little bit, or you nudge the tempo knob on the drum machine...end of overdub session. The solution is to *record the master clock signal on tape*, and then while overdubbing, slave all devices to this pre-recorded clock signal. (Note: The signal coming from the tape is not sufficiently clean for most purposes, so this approach requires some signal conditioning in order to turn the taped signal into a waveform suitable for use as a clock signal. Devices with sync-to-tape include such a conditioner.) As with our previous examples, all devices must start at the beginning of the tune. One master clock pulse looks like any other to the slaves, so the slaves have no way of knowing whether the pulse currently being received is the 10th or 10000th...unless, of course, they started counting these pulses from the very first pulse. What this means is that if you want to overdub the last two measures of a song, you still have to start at the beginning and amuse yourself until the last two measures roll by.

Unfortunately, recording clock pulses on tape is not particularly reliable. After shuttling tape around for a while, occasionally some tape oxide will shed off and create a dropout, thus eliminating a pulse or two from the clock track. If you try to overdub an instrument to this messed up clock track, sync will not be maintained with tracks which had been synched to the clock track before the dropout occurred.

Many manufacturers chose *FSK synchronization* as a more reliable sync-to-tape method. Instead of simply recording on-off clock pulses on tape, this sync system shifts between two different frequencies (hence the term Frequency Shift Keying). Tape is much happier recording alternating audio tones than clock pulses, and this system is also somewhat less sensitive to dropouts. Unfortunately, each manufacturer has their own standard. So, if you put a Linn sync track down on tape, you cannot sync a Roland or Oberheim drum unit to that same track. However, since many units have external clock outputs and inputs, you can do some roundabout tricks. For example, a drum unit could sync to the FSK track, then its clock output could drive another

Fig. 3   Note Resolutions in 24 ppqn

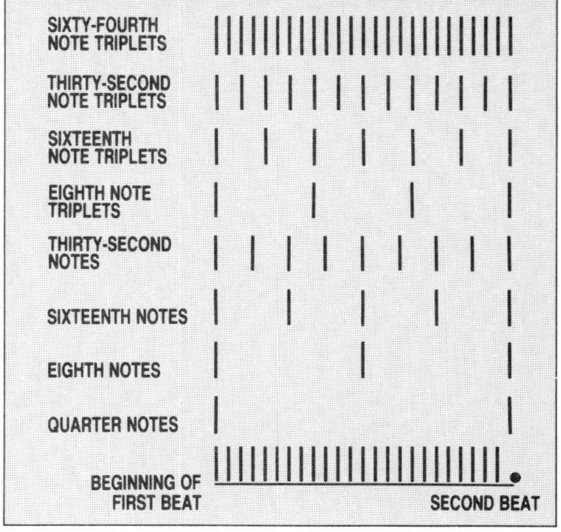

unit's clock input (see Fig. 4). Still, you could run into the problem where one unit requires a different clock rate from another.

When enough musicians get frustrated, someone else sees a product: about the same time I designed the Master Synchronizer for budget sync applications, Garfield Electronics introduced the Doctor Click for high-end sync applications. Intended as a universal clock transmitter/receiver/translator, Doctor Click lets you take a sync track (recorded on tape or "live") and translate it to just about any other format. You could even take a "click track" (metronome signal recorded on tape) and synthesize a sync track at the proper rate—24, 48, or 96 ppqn. [*The Doctor Click was also able to calibrate in frames per beat, making it far more affordable for film scorers to synchronize to a metronome beat, or "sync to click." In the decades previous to the Doctor Click, soundtrackers were limited to the ultra-expensive Urei 964*].

Although problem solver boxes such as the Doctor Click were very useful, they were still band-aid solutions: The underlying problem, lack of standards and design incompatibility, remained...thus giving impetus to MIDI's creation.

Midi Synchronization.

MIDI, a computer "language" designed to allow computer-controlled instruments to communicate with each other, was designed to handle system synchronization as well as functions such as note messages, instrument dynamics, etc. MIDI specifies a 24 ppqn clock system, so that means no more incompatible clock rates between manufacturers. MIDI also provides several other timing related "messages" that can be exchanged between machines (typically from the master to the slave). These include:

Start. When the master transmits a start message over MIDI (usually initiated by pressing the Play switch), all slaves instantly reset themselves to the beginning of the song and start counting along with the MIDI clock signal.

Stop. When the master transmits a stop message, everything stops counting.

Continue. Continue tells the slaves to pick up from wherever they were when the stop message was sent.

Song Position Pointer. A MIDI sequencer or drum machine can keep track of how many measures (up to a maximum of 1024 measures) have elapsed since the sequence was started. This is a very powerful feature: for example, suppose that a sequencer capable of sending measure information feeds a drum machine capable of receiving measure information. If you select a certain measure number on the master as the start point, both units will automatically position themselves at the beginning of that measure. Tell them to start by pushing the Play button, and they will start together from the same measure and count at the same rate. Once started, they remain in sync by virtue of being driven by the same timing reference.

A word of caution: Remember that not all MIDI instruments include the same complement of features, so some slaves may not be able to accept song position pointer data. Make sure you check units for compatibility (refer to each device's MIDI Implementation Sheet) before expecting to use them in a system context.

Synchronizing MIDI Devices to Tape Via SMPTE.

Synchronizing MIDI devices, especially sequencers, to tape gives amazing flexibility: You can record electronic MIDI instruments on the MIDI sequencer and acoustic instruments on the multi-track recorder, then during mixdown synchronize the two together to obtain more tracks than you could have from the tape recorder alone. The tracks recorded in the sequencer are often called "virtual tracks," since they fulfill the exact same function as tracks recorded on tape—yet are not recorded on tape.

Many sequencers have sync-to-tape facilities built-in, which certainly makes life convenient. In fact, for most synchronization applications, the sequencer's sync-to-tape is all you'll ever need. These days, though, life does not involve only audio; there's also video, and we might want to sync a sequencer, audio recorder, and video recorder together...which brings us to SMPTE (Society of Motion Picture and Television Engineers) time code.

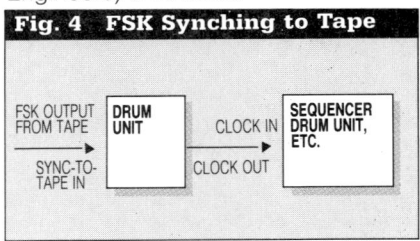

Fig. 4 FSK Synching to Tape

All About SMPTE.

Although we've already covered several timing standards, for most professional videotape editing and multitrack synchronization applications SMPTE time code is the sync standard of choice. Originally developed by NASA as a means of accurately logging data, SMPTE time code labels each frame of a videotape or film by recording a unique piece of digital data on that frame. For American (NTSC standard) television and video, each second of SMPTE time code is divided into 30 frames (the standard number of frames that pass by in one second of video; the standard frame rate for film is 24 frames per second, and for European television and video, 25 frames per second). Each frame is further divided into 80 subframes, with each subframe being a little less than half a millisecond long. A typical time code location might be 00:10:08:29:(76), which you would read as 00 hours, 10 minutes, 8 seconds, 29 frames, and 76 subframes into the videotape. SMPTE also provides for "user bits" so that users can include custom pieces of data in the time code.

The SMPTE time code emanating from a SMPTE generator can be recorded onto one track of tape, thus serving the function of a super-accurate index counter. Instead of having to rely on some external mechanical thing that slips and has no real relationship to the tape, timing information is preserved *on the tape itself*. This data can then be played back into a SMPTE time code reader which precisely identifies where you are on the tape. SMPTE time code not only helps synchronize audio to video, but can also synchronize two or more audio recorders together—as well as some other tricks that we'll mention later on.

The best news for musicians is that there are now several SMPTE-to-MIDI synchronizers that correlate MIDI song position data to SMPTE time code readings. For example, suppose that measure 16 of a song (which marks, say, the beginning of the chorus) starts at SMPTE 00:00:45:(10), and measure 24 (which marks the beginning of the second verse) starts at SMPTE 00:01:10: (15). If you roll tape starting at 00:00:45:(10), the synchronizer box will send out MIDI data that tells the slave units to start at measure 24. Of course, starting the tape in different places will send out different song position information. Therefore, you can roll tape at any point and within a fraction of a second, any sequencer or drum machine that responds to song position pointer information will "know" where it should be in the sequence relative to the time code, and start playing at that measure.

Usually the beginning of the SMPTE time code is not at the same point as the beginning of the composition, since it's good practice to include an "electronic leader" of time code (when synchronizing tape machines, this gives plenty of time for them to overcome any mechanical inertia and sync up). To compensate for this leader, as well as to overcome other problems, most synchronizers (such as Roland's SBX-80) include *offset registers* which will cause MIDI timing information to start only when the SMPTE reader reaches a specified number.

Of course, you don't always need fancy tools to perform SMPTE-to-MIDI

sync. As mentioned earlier, Frank Serafine synchronizes SMPTE and MIDI by simply recording two sync tracks, one with MIDI-compatible clock information and one with SMPTE timing information, on adjacent tracks of a multi-track recorder. Thus, the two timing tracks are always in sync with each other, and he can relate the MIDI timing information to SMPTE timing information recorded on the next track over. This approach does use up two tracks, but is very reliable and saves the cost of a synchronizer box.

So now our MIDI system is synched up to SMPTE...but there's more.

SMPTE – Reading Instruments.

Some instruments can optionally bypass MIDI and sync directly to SMPTE. E-mu's Emulator II, for example, can both read and write SMPTE time code as well as follow MIDI timing messages. You can specify a sequence start point in SMPTE time code, which is of tremendous use in video work: Suppose you're adding one minute worth of sound effects in the middle of a video—say, starting at SMPTE time code 01:05:10:(77)—and you have the Emulator synched up to the SMPTE time code recorded on the video's control track. You can sample the needed sound effects into the Emulator II, start the sequencer at SMPTE 01:05:10:(77), then play each sound effect into the sequencer while watching the video action. Rewind the video to just before the start point, enter the SMPTE time code value where you want the sequencer to start playback—in this case, SMPTE 01:05:10:(77)—and what the sequence plays will be in sync with the visuals.

The Emulator II also provides a sort of "chase" function. If you roll tape and the SMPTE time code is prior to the sequencer start point, the Emulator II will wait for the tape to catch up. If the SMPTE time code is later than the sequencer start point the Emulator II will "fast-forward" through its sequence in order to catch up to the time code.

SMPTE Tape Control.

SMPTE can also help automate tape control functions. For example, the SMPL system from Synchronous Technologies lets you specify punch-in and punch-out points in relation to SMPTE time code. Thus, once you've entered the punch-in and punch-out

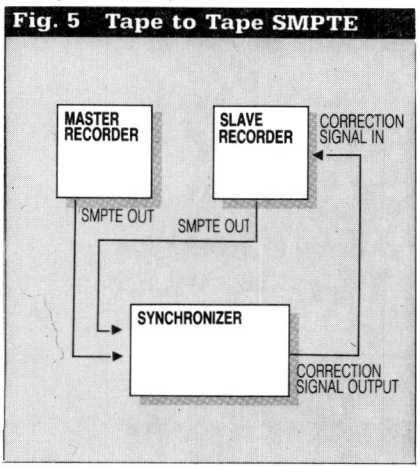

Fig. 5   Tape to Tape SMPTE

MASTER RECORDER

SLAVE RECORDER

CORRECTION SIGNAL IN

SMPTE OUT

SMPTE OUT

SYNCHRONIZER

CORRECTION SIGNAL OUTPUT

time code values, SMPL takes over from there. SMPL also allows for auto-location. If you want to go to the tape position indicated by time code 00:05:12:13 (the basic SMPL system doesn't use subframes), SMPL will first put the recorder into play and read the time code to determine the present position of the tape. Next, SMPL will use its knowledge of the transport mechanics to rewind or fast forward to within a few seconds of the auto-locate point, and then "park" within 15 to 29 frames prior to the specified auto-locate point. For use with master clock based systems, SMPL will also provide a 24, 48, or 96 ppqn signal synchronized to SMPTE. This signal always begins on the next metronome beat following a cue point (specified with SMPTE time code) to maintain rhythmic consistency. (Note: A chase lock accessory adds SMPTE-to-MIDI translation and machine-to-machine synchronization, the subject of our next section.)

Machine-to-Machine Sync with SMPTE.

Before MIDI sequencers and drum machines became so important, SMPTE's main audio use was to synchronize two recorders via an expensive *chase-locking* synchronizer, so called because the synchronizer causes the slave to "chase" the master and "lock" to the master's time code. Both the master and the slave must have SMPTE time code recorded on one track; when the tape is rolling, this data feeds into the synchronizer. The synchronizer reads the time code from the two machines and compares them. If the slave is running a little slow or fast compared to the master, the synchronizer sends an appropriate correction signal to the slave so that the two machines maintain sync (see Fig. 5).

Machine-to-machine sync has several applications. One is to lock two multi-track machines together to obtain more tracks (i.e. two 24-tracks slaved together to give 48 tracks total, of which two are dedicated to time code). Another is to create "slave reels" in order to avoid playing a master tape too many times. Once the rhythm tracks are recorded on the master machine, these tracks can be premixed to one or two tracks on the slave machine. Overdubs are then added to the reel on the slave machine. Once overdubs are complete, the slave and master machines are synched together, and

the overdubbed parts are transferred over to the master reel.

A final SMPTE application involves "pyramiding," as used by synthesist Larry Fast (Synergy and Peter Gabriel band). He prefers to work at home on his 8-track, but in many cases needs more than eight tracks to complete a project. So, he records SMPTE on one track of the 8-track, then fills up the other tracks with parts. After recording the tracks he books some time at House of Music (a 24-track studio) and transfers the tracks, including SMPTE, over to the 24-track. He then syncs the 24-track and 8-track together, makes a pre-mix from the 24 on to one track of the 8-tracks, goes home, and loads up the remaining six tracks on his 8-track. He then books some more time, syncs the 24-track and 8-track machines together, transfers his new overdubs, and so on until all 24 tracks are filled up. Not only does he get to work at home, but this saves a lot of money; the time required to transfer the parts is minimal, so the only significant studio cost is for mixdown time.

Wrapping Up...

In today's audio/video studio, SMPTE provides the system master clock, while MIDI acts as an intelligent interface between various pieces of equipment. Synchro-sonic triggers and pulses can further be derived from MIDI to trigger individual events, or provide compatibility with older gate- and trigger-oriented systems. All in all, there are a lot of ways to synchronize devices.

Everything is not perfectly rosy, however. Many SMPTE/MIDI devices are expensive, and each one seems to have some particular feature not shared by the others...So shop very carefully before laying down your bucks. Also, different devices take different amounts of time to process the SMPTE or MIDI signal. As a result, some instruments may lag behind other instruments by a few milliseconds; these errors are often tuned out using delay lines, or delay facilities built into the synchronizers themselves.

But most problems are surmountable, and besides, synchronization is a relatively new subject, so some growing pains are inevitable. As the music industry becomes more sync-conscious, it won't be long before we start to see signal processors, mixers and other devices that can read SMPTE time code directly. Truly low-cost automated mixdown is not far away either, and some advanced SMPTE-ready devices are available now (such as TASCAM's Model 58 recorder, and the new Fostex two-track that includes a center-channel third track for recording time code). Learning to apply synchronizers has improved my efficiency in the studio, allowed for more sophisticated musical compositions, and opened up the world of video/audio production...spend a little time delving into the subject, and your horizons will be broadened as well.

Craig Anderton, a.k.a. Captain MIDI, is a noted inventor and educator and now editor of Electronic Musician.

The Well-Tempered Computer Family

How the Hell Did All These Computers Get in My Studio?
By Freff.

In my hard-won studio there are many tools: guitars and basses, microphones and mixers, signal processors and synths. And four computers. *Four* computers? (Six, actually, if you count the two I keep down the hall.) For a recording studio that used to be a modestly-proportioned bedroom? How the hell did this happen?

Flippant answer: one by one. Real answer: because they do the jobs I need done, and they do them superbly. I wouldn't be helpless without them, certainly not that . . . but I'd have a damn sight less power at my disposal. And with them, this once-upon-a-bedroom can hold its own with the most sophisticated recording studios in the world.

Think that's hype? I call it heaven. Come meet my microcomputer family and decide for yourself.

Computer #1: GRANDPA

THE APPLE II–PLUS: 64K of RAM, two disc drives, Sakata color monitor, various peripheral cards, extended game paddle port and a variety of joysticks to choose from.

This was my first computer, and I have an incredibly soft spot in my heart for it. The disc drives should probably be replaced, and 64K isn't much memory, and I've never been sure exactly what color it is (other than not quite beige and not quite green) . . . but oh, what unexpected doors it opened.

They began opening five years ago, when I was trying to borrow a typewriter. An engineer friend—with all the calculation of a pusher eyeing a likely target— loaned me his thoroughly customized Apple II, an early word-processing program, and a used teletype loud enough to drown out thunderstorms. In two weeks I wrote what normally would have taken me two months. Did I call him a pusher? Call me an addict. I was *hooked*.

In 1981 I got my own Apple, from the first computer store to open in Manhattan. The complete setup, with software and dot matrix printer and all the expensive bells and whistles set me back over five thousand dollars. I stayed with Apple for two reasons. First, there wasn't a lot of choice in those days— remember, this was eons before you could buy a computer at K-Mart for less than good seats at a Prince concert. Second, and more important, *an Apple could be used for music*. It had a built-in speaker, there were these digital oscillator cards you could buy for it, and . . . well, if this thing could bleep on cue, I was for it. As it happened, it did a lot more than just bleep; which is why it now lives nestled comfortably in my studio, in the keyboard racks, below the CAT SRM II and above the DX7, lid removed for easy access and maximum air cooling.

I use it in five ways.

First, it's the heart of my alphaSyntauri system. This is a hardware/software combination that turns the Apple into a digital synthesizer with sixteen oscillators, a five-octave keyboard, the capacity for microtonal scales, and a 16 track sequencer. The sound is a bit thin in character and needs a lot of signal processing to work on tape, but there are pluses enough to balance the scale, like neat special effects and the fact that it can generate eight different timbres simultaneously (add in the sequencer and you've got a powerful tool for sketching out orchestrations). I wouldn't trade or sell mine. It also illustrates an interesting phenomenon of life in these computer times, a sort of *pseudo*-obsolescence. The Syntauri Corporation itself is dead and gone. Look for it in data heaven. But there is still plenty of alphaSyntauri-related software and hardware being developed, by both the original design-

ers (most of whom now work for a music software company called Mimetics) and talented users. The company is dead, but the instrument lives on, and actually improves. It didn't used to work like that!

My Apple's second use is that of music tutor. There are over fifty different theory programs available on the market today, covering topics from sight reading to ear training, at levels of complexity from kindergarten to college. It's nice to be able to study at my own rate, and the programs that take an arcade-style approach are a nice break from routine. (Avoid any ear training programs that use the Apple's own speaker instead of an external synth, though.)

Third use is as a controller for my Drumulator, using E-mu's GRC (Graphic Rhythm Composer) program. I find this more flexible and expressive than programming patterns from the drum machine's front panel...especially when going for those quirks of timing and volume changes that humanize a track.

Fourth use is as a programmer and librarian for my Yamaha DX7. If you've ever tried to edit voices on a DX7, you know how crazy the single data slider

and little display can make you. Tackling the task with a computer keyboard and full-screen color graphics is a whole different story. In fact, right now I'm using four different Apple/DX7 programs, trying to decide which combination I like best.

They're all basically good and useful; choosing between them comes down to a matter of personal style. Yamaha's DX-PRO has got a great visual interface that makes voice design easy to understand. But on my computer, at least, the program is quirky. Cherry Lane's DX-HEAVEN has simpler graphics that pack more voice parameters onto a single screen. Some people will like seeing everything at once; others might find all the numbers a bit overwhelming. Then there is Mimetics' DATA-7, less a programmer than a good analyzer; you still have to do all your editing from the DX7 itself. The computer just makes it easier to see what's going on.

A bonus with all these programs is that they let you store your DX7 voices on floppy discs. Keeping a voice library using RAM cartridges is expensive, what with every 32-voice cartridge costing you $90. But a floppy disc only costs $2 to $3 and stores *800* voices.

Which brings me to Mimetics' PERFORMANCE-7, a stage and studio godsend for any DX7 owner with a good voice library. PERFORMANCE-7 does one thing, and one thing only. It keeps ten different banks—320 voices—instantly available. To load a new bank you just tap a number on the Apple keyboard and wait a couple of seconds.

Lastly, my Apple becomes part of the studio MIDI network whenever I run MIDI/4, a 4-track recording program from Passport Systems. Frankly, that isn't very often these days. MIDI/4 is a simple, solid program that gives good service for a reasonable price. But it is limited by the Apple itself, which doesn't have enough memory to run the *really* hot MIDI recording packages.

#2: JUNIOR
The SMPLE SYSTEM: Commodore VIC-20 converted by Synchronous Technologies of Oklahoma City, Oklahoma.
One interface card and Zenith monochrome green monitor.

Nobody takes a Commodore VIC-20 seriously. It's a toy computer, designed for and sold in a kiddie computer marketplace that wasn't even dreamed of in the days I bought my Apple. But the fact is even this "toy" computer has a lot of power when properly tapped. You just have to see the potential.

John Simonton, of PAIA and Synchronous Technologies, had his eyes open. And so he created his SMPL System around a heavily converted VIC-20, in one sweep making SMPTE and computerized tape recording affordable for people with less than astronomical budgets. Like me.

Basic operation is very simple. I start by using the SMPL unit to lay down a track of SMPTE timecode on my 8-track. From then on I can ignore the transport controls on the Otari and operate everything from SMPL. It reads the timecode on the tape and uses it as a guide for both auto-location and automatic

Can a full-service computer studio survive in Brooklyn?
Yes, with good locks.

punch-in and punch-out. The effect is eerie. SMPL is always accurate, but at the beginning of a session is takes time searching for its marks. This search time gets shorter as the session progresses, until it's almost nonexistent and SMPL is whizzing right along. It's like having the Invisible Man for an assistant engineer, doing perfect punches for you from across the room. SMPL also sends out sync pulses in 24-, 48- or 96-pulse formats, to drive drum machines and—if you have the right interface—MIDI sequencers.

SMPL costs about $1,000. And coming out sometime now is an expanded interface with MIDI, simultaneous and separate sync outputs, plus the ability to do gen-lock and chase-lock with separate recorders, or a recorder and a VCR...for only $500 more.

#3: THE TRANSIENT COUSIN

THE APPLE MACINTOSH: sometimes 128K of RAM, sometimes 512K, external disc drives, Imagewriter printer.

Macintoshes come and go around here, usually rented. I don't own one yet and I'm not really sure I want to, not until they do something about that incredibly slow and annoying Disc Operating System. My old Apple II-Plus is faster. (If you're thinking of buying a Macintosh, for heaven's sake don't do it unless you get the 512K version with an external disc drive.) But I do have to admit I like the two musical programs I've run on it.

The first is called MUSICWORKS, from MacroMind. It's pure fun. Somewhat limited, because it generates sound with the Macintosh oscillators instead of external synths, but a MIDI version is supposed to be in the works. In the meantime, the musical graphics are superb and you can get some interesting accidental compositions by sweeping the computer's mouse around at random. A good buy for its $49.95 price.

Not nearly so inexpensive is the MACATTACH communications package for the Kurzweil 250. But then, before you even need the $1,800-plus Mac and the $150-plus software, you'll have already spent somewhere between fourteen and sixteen thousand on your K250 (with sampling option). What's a couple thousand more? MACATTACH is the software that coordinates data transfer between the K250 and a Macintosh disc, so you'll need it to build your own library of sounds.

More exciting for the Mac are two programs that are just now making an

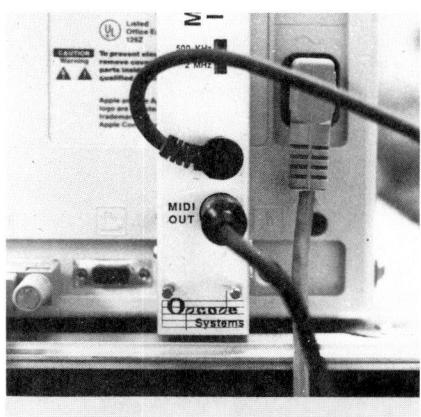

Opcode MIDIMAC interface.

impact on the industry: SOUND DESIGNER from Digidesign for the Emulator II, and Southworth Music's TOTAL MUSIC. TOTAL MUSIC is an extremely comprehensive MIDI hardware/software package, judging from specs and some advance demos I've seen. And SOUND DESIGNER makes an Emulator II act like a Fairlight CMI for about a third the total price. (A new program for the Apple makes similarly incredible enhancements to the Ensoniq Mirage sampler.) If these live up to advance word, I may buy a Macintosh yet.

#4: ALL-KNOWING FATHER FIGURE

THE IBM PC: 640K of RAM, two disc drives, Hercules Graphic Card, Amdek monochrome amber monitor, Roland MPU-401 MIDI interface.

This computer is my favorite. Power is up and price is down. Mine only cost $2,800. It is common to sneer at the IBM PC and its parent company in some computer circles. But the hardware itself is perfectly respectable, and in any case the real question is always software, software, software: are the *programs* out there?

Well, let's see....

I'm using XYWRITE II-PLUS for word-processing right now. (Word-processing isn't musical? I write song lyrics on it—that counts.) I'm using DBASE III for my databases. What good are they in a studio? Plenty. They're invaluable for keeping track charts, tape catalogs, synthesizer voicing data sheets, equipment maintenance schedules, musician contact lists and expenses.

There's only one synth programmer/librarian so far, a program for my Voyetra 8 from Octave Plateau. I'm hoping for CZ-101 and DX7 programs for the

PC, someday, but there are none out yet. (A good CZ-101 programmer for the Apple, by the way, is Cherry Lane's CZ-RIDER.) This is an excellent argument for two computers in the studio, incidentally—one is always free for sequencing when the other is voice-editing.

But wonderful though all of these are, they wouldn't be enough to replace the old Apple in my estimation. Except, see, there are these three devastating MIDI recording programs....

In order of release they are Jim Miller's PERSONAL COMPOSER, Octave Plateau's SEQUENCER PLUS, and Cherry Lane's TEXTURE, written by Utopia's Roger Powell. Although they all work though the Roland MPU-401, each takes a totally different approach to the problems of multitrack MIDI recording. As a result, I find all three useful at different times, and haven't got a clear favorite.

PERSONAL COMPOSER's strong suit is notation. It works in several ways. On one side, you can write actual scores on the computer screen, scores of up to orchestral complexity, using a mouse or the computer's keyboard, and when you are done that score can drive a network of MIDI synths. If you put in *The Rite Of Spring*, by God, *The Rite Of Spring* is what you hear played back. Also well-organized is a 32-track sequencer. But the most interesting features in the program are still taking shape. Ready for this? You can MIDI-record a keyboard performance and have PERSONAL COMPOSER *convert that into music notation.* I could give music printouts from this program to session players without the slightest hesitation. It's very clean. And coming in future versions is something called "midigraphics," which will let you create your own notation characters, assign MIDI meanings to them, and then use them in your own scores.

TEXTURE takes an approach Roger Powell calls "modular recording." Using it to compose is like constructing a mosaic—you build up larger pieces from the selected repetition of smaller fragments. Each song can have up to sixty-four "links" made up of different combinations of sixty-four different "patterns," arranged over eight tracks. I haven't had this program long, but I'm finding it quite pleasing to work with.

SEQUENCER PLUS' strong point is *control*—no, make that CONTROL! It has sixty-four tracks for recording, with room for around 60,000 notes in a 640K IBM PC like mine, and every single one of those 60,000 notes can be edited for length, pitch, start time, volume...even release velocity, if you have synths which use that data, like Prophet T8s and Chromas do. Music is notated in graphic form, as bars on a grid. The higher the bar, the higher the pitch. The longer the bar, the longer the note. It's such a simple interface that its power is not immediately apparent, but after a short time you'll likely find standard notation stiff and a little disappointing to work with. I know I do.

In addition, it can be synched to tape through the MPU-401 (or SMPL, using a Nano Doc from Garfield Electronics.) In my studio this has two immediate and overwhelming benefits. First, I'm not limited to eight tracks anymore. Instead I have seven "acoustic" tracks to record on with microphones, one for the sync code, and then *up to sixty-four MIDI synth tracks that will always be in sync with the miked stuff.* Suppose I make a tape recording and a MIDI-recording simultaneously. Three days later I change my mind about something, maybe a note or a timbre. All I have to do is edit the computer score, sync the computer and the tape back together, hook up the synth of my choice, and drop the new track perfectly into place. Even total garbage can be edited into perfection if you take the time.

#?: THE NEXT GENERATION

THE SOMETHING THAT HASN'T BEEN BUILT YET: more memory, more speed, better graphics, more POWER.

Right now I'm surrounded by networks. There's the network that feeds the patchbay for the recording chain, the patchbay made up of instrument outputs, the MIDI net, and all the various control systems. I've arranged my little room so that I can sit in a couple of different places and reach the three or four control panels that *count*—the PC keyboard, SMPL, the Otari recording remote, any (or all) of my MIDI synths I can hold in my lap—and that's wonderful.

But gosh, if I just had a little more computer power, and more of the signal-processing gear had interface jacks built in, and the networks could be merged into one...oh my. Oh my my.

MIDI Product Directory.

Compiled by Will Hunt.

MIDI Synthesizers

● **Yamaha**	**CP7**	61 keys, 2 piano 2 harpsichord voices, stereo chorus, built-in speakers.	**$445**
	PF10	FM digital piano, 76 keys, velocity sensitive, built-in speakers.	**$1595**
	DX21	FM digital synthesizer, 61 keys, 8 note polyphonic, 128 patches.	**$795**
	DX9	FM, 6 operators, 32 algorithms, 16-voice	
	DX7	FM digital, touch sensitive, external memories, you've heard of this one.	**$1995**
	DX5	More and fancier. Split keyboards, scaling control, velocity, aftertouch, foot switching, more voice & function parameters.	**$3,495**
	DXI	Top of da line. Yamaha say "The most sophisticated digital synthesizer available." Who am I to squawk?	**$10,900**
	TXI	Basic FM rack-mount module. 6 operators, 32 algorithms, programmable via MIDI.	**$545**
	TX7	Expander module: a DX7 without the keyboard.	**$845**
	TX 216	Two DX7s in a box.	**$2,095**
		Extra TFI modules to beef up your TX 216	**$545**
	TX816 Tone Generator System	Eight DX7s independently accessible. Note limit function can confine each voice to a particular area of a simple MIDI keyboard. An enormously powerful setup.	**$4,995**
● **Casio**	**CZ-101**	8-voice polyphonic. Puts ASDR to shame with an eight-stage envelope generator. Has tone mixing. Sounds great. Tricky to program. An amazing introduction. Tiny keys, RAM cartridge. MIDI in/out.	**$499**
	CZ-1000	It's a CZ-101 with full-size keys.	**$699**
	CZ-3000	A CZ-5000 without the sequencer.	**$999**
	CZ-5000	61 full size keys, 16 voice polyphonic, built-in sequencer, tape memory storage. MIDI through as well as MIDI in/out.	**$1,199**
	CT-6000	Touch sensitive, 20 preset sounds, auto-accompaniment, chord memory, MIDI-off feature for lower keys. Home-organ version. Casio's sounds are made with phase distortion synthesis. Suffice to say it's different from anyone else's, and it sounds excellent.	**$999**
● **Roland**	**Juno 106**	6-voice polyphonic, has knobs and sliders. Eureka! Good sounds. User-friendly, but digitally correct.	**$1,095**
	JX-3P	64 patches, 6 voice polyphonic, sequencer with tape storage, optional PG-200 programmer available too.	**$1,395**
	JX-8P	Pressure/velocity sensitive, digitally programmed. Nice, nice sounds. 64 presets, 32 programmable patches, memory cartridge.	**$1,695**
	PG-800	Programming module for JX8P—plug it in & you've got knobs & faders! Death to step-programming.	**$295**
	Jupiter-6	6-voice polyphonic, lots of split-keyboard options, cassette-interface, 2 VCOs per voice. Arpeggiator. Roland has kept to analog synthesis, while using digital controls. This makes for nice, warm sounds and quick, easy patching.	**$2,995**
	EP-50 electronic piano	76 keys, touch sensitive, 8-voice polyphonic MIDI controller, built-in speakers, 3 piano, 1 harpsichord sound, chorus, key-transpose.	**$795**
	Synth Plus-60 (HS-60)	6-voice polyphonic, built-in speakers, chorus, volume pedal, portamento, 128 patches. Built for people who distrust amplifiers?	**$1,095**

	Piano Plus-400 (HP-400)	88 keys, elecronic piano with MIDI	**$1495**
	Piano Plus-300 (HP-300)	75 keys, electronic piano with MIDI.	**$1,295**
● Korg	**Poly 61M**	6-voice polyphonic, 64 programs, sequencer, editing. Retro-fit kit available for pre-MIDI Poly 61S.	
	Poly 800	8-voice, 6-stage envelope, 49 full-size keys, lots of good little stuff.	**$795**
	Poly 800 Mark II	Includes MIDI refinements, programmable digital delay	
	EX 800	Expander module—Poly 800. Brains without the keyboard—for MIDI of course.	**$395**
	RK-100	Controller	**$995**
	DW 6000	61 keys, digital/analog hybrid. Unique sound, digital advantages, MIDI in/out/through.	
	DW 8000	Five octaves, weighted keys, fully touch sensitive, built-in digital delay—wow.	**$1,195**
	EX 8000	Rack mount brains of DW 8000	**$995**
● Sequential Circuits	**Six Trak**	6-voice polyphonic, it's a six-channel multitrack recorder, multi-timbral, with a sequencer in it! for only...	**$895**
	Max	6-voice multi-timbral, one VCO per voice, sequencer inboard—cheap! A good MIDI module.	**$599**
	Multi-Trak	See Of Plugs and Bugs, p.48.	**$1499**
	Prophet 600	A sequencer on board, analog controls, digital memory, those Prophet sounds....	**$1,195**
	Prophet T8	8-voice polyphonic, weighted, velocity-sensitive keyboard,(used in the Synclavier). 128 patches, Prophet sounds. Keys also measure *release* velocity, for a third expression option.	**$5,895**
	Split-8	8-voice polyphonic, split keyboard capabilities Sequential Circuits, 3051 North First St., San Jose, CA 95134. (408) 946-5240.	**$1199**
● Europa	**Oscar**	Ugly little monophonic with 1500-note digital sequencing, MIDI in/out/through, hot bass sounds. Digital Oscillators, low, mid, hi-pass filters. Contact Europa Technology. (See Lync keyboard controller).	**$995**
● Fender	**Chroma Polaris**	6-voice, 61-note velocity-sensitive weighted keys. 132 programs in memory plus 132 offloaded in cassette. Sequencer onboard, lots of great unique features.	**$1,495**
● Oberheim	**Matrix-6**	6-voice analog, velocity/after touch, keyboard split, footpedal, footswitch, assignable controllers 100 single patches or 50 multi.	**$1,595**
	Xpander	See MIDI modules	**$2,995**
	OB-8	8-voice, 120 patches, very classy analog	**$4,545**
	Matrix-12	6! keys, velocity and pressure sensitive, the equivalent of two Xpanders. Very sophisticated analog synth.	**$4,995**
● Digital Keyboards	**Synergy**	74 keys, 32 oscillators, 2, 3, or 4 per key. Additive synthesis, phase modulation and cancellation (sort of like FM but different). Velocity sensitive, sequencer. Computer aided for extensive voice editing.	**$5,295**
● P.P.G. Wave	**Wave 2.3**	8 digital channels with analog controls, pressure-sensitive keyboard, controls volume, filter, and wavetable. Big, complicated, wonderful, nobody knows how it works.	**$8,995**
	PRK	Optional six octave, weighted wooden keys.	**$2,995**
● Technics	**SX-K350**	Onboard 4 channel sequencer, PCM synthesis.	
Kawai	**SX-240**	8-voice, split keyboards, sequencer, footswitch controls, clock in/out. You can name your patches with letters!	**$1,295**
● Solton	**Project 100**	6-voice polyphonic, 40 presets, 60 programmable sounds, cassette memory storage. Chorus, release pedal, 16 measure sequencer.	
	Programmer 24	Rhythm programmer, bass sequencer-rhythm section in a box, live playing possible. Pedalboard. This is either awesome or really tacky. I can't tell.	
	SM 1000	Project 100 guts in a box with little rubber feet. Would fall out of a rack. How do I know what it sounds like? MIDI in MIDI out MIDI through, tape interface. Solton Music GmbH, Gewerbering 31, D-8398 Pocking. W. Germany. Tel. 0531-4038. Telex 57605 Solton I.	
● Octave Plateau	**Voyetra Eight**	Synth in rackmount module, controller separate. 8-voice analog. Velocity/pressure sensitive. Joystick, 4 control directions, programmable footpedal and footswitch options. Arpeggiator, polyphonic sequencer, keyboard splits and layering. MIDI	**$4,595**

		in/out/through from the rack.	
		Keyboard	$995
● Akai	AX-80	8-voice, touch sensitive, 96 patches, 61 keys, velocity sensitive, 32 presets, cassette storage MIDI in/out/through.	$595
		Akai, Box 2344, Forth Worth, TX 76113. (817) 336-5114.	
● BIT	One	61 keys, 6-voice, velocity sensitive, 63 patch memory, cassette storage, unique sound.	$1,396
Suzuki	Keyman	Inexpensive digital synthesizers with lots of little features. Auto-accompaniment, keyboard split, arpeggiators, 1-finger chord play, built-in speakers. Who knows? Maybe they sound o.k. MIDI one up to your Synclavier.	$179 to $599
		Suzuki Corporation, P.O. Box 261030, San Diego, CA 92126.	
● Siel	MK-490	Digital, built-in sequencer, one finger chord play.	$299
	MK-610	& a built-in demo song!	$310
	PX-JR	Touch sensitive piano, built-in speaker.	$595
	DK-600	61 keys, 6-voice, velocity sensitive, good metallic sounds.	$1,295
	Expander	DK 600 in a box, enables split of DK 600 keyboard, double the sounds.	$795
		Music Technology, 105 Fifth Avenue, Garden City Park, NY 11040. (516) 747-7890.	
● Hohner	PK250	61 note keyboard, 32 polyphonic and solo voices, arranger program, Multiple Event Generator sound generation system. probably unique. Try one.	$1,695
		Hohner Inc., Lakeridge Park, Sycamore Dr., Ashland, VA 23005.	
● Seiko	DS-250	Two 8-note polyphonic sound sources, 6 waveforms, detune split keyboard, chorus, transpose. But again...those built-in speakers! Makes you wonder if they're serious. But wait...two 8-note independent sound generators? With three split points? Check this out.	$599.50
	DS-310	Plug-in module. User programming of DS-250. Waveform modifications, ADSR, 4 sound memories, 4 envelope patterns.	$249.50
		Kaman Music Distibutors, P.O. Box 507, Bloomfield CT 06002.	
● WERSI		German instruments. You can put them together yourself! A strange combination super-organ digital dinosaur. Voicings look quite flexible. Send for the brochure. It says they do it all.	
	MK-1	8 addressable MIDI channels, DMS Multi Processor system. Cartridge memories.	
		Kit:	$1,850
		Assembled:	$2,450
	Condor	16-note polyphonic, digital voice design with computer interfacing.	
		Kit:	$1,950
		Assembled:	$2,950
		For WERSI see MIDI organs.	
● Moog	Memory Moog Plus	6-voice, polyphonic, 100 presets, 3 oscillators per voice cassette dump—good for strings, a polyphonic descendant of the Mini-Moog.	$1,195
		Moog Electronics, 2500 Walden Ave., Buffalo, NY 14225	

MIDI Keyboard Controllers

● Korg	RK-100	41-key strap-on, 3 controls on the neck, pitch-bend, volume modulation. 64 patches, 4-colors.	$495
● Yamaha	KX5	37 keys, strap-on, velocity and pressure-sensitive. Ribbon controller, battery powered, mini keys.	$495
	KX-1	Strap-on, full-size keys, velocity and pressure-sensitive, ribbon controller. More controls.	$1,295
	KX88	88 full-size, weighted keys, 19 types of controls, breath control, aftertouch, and modulation wheel control.	$1,695
● Oberheim	XK	61 keys, 2 MIDI outs, split keyboard, arpeggiator, pressure and velocity sensitive, weighs 15 pounds!	$995
● LYNC	Remote Keyboard	4-octave, programmable velocity sensitive, strap-on, 64 patch memories, each stores info for 4 external synths thru 4 MIDI channels.	$1,295

Europa Technology, 1638 W. Washington Blvd., Venice, CA 90291.

● Roland	Axis-1	45 key strap-on, Velocity, pressure sensitive, Poly or Mono chord memory, transposition, 120 patch memories.	$695
	MKB-200	61 weighted, velocity/pressure sensitive, 2 MIDI outs, split keyboard possible.	$995
	MKB-300	76 organ-type keys, 4 MIDI outs, Poly or Mono velocity sensitive, split-keyboard, or dual mode, 128 patch memories, battery memory backup. Damper pedal, soft pedal.	$1,295
	MKB-1000	88 weighted keys, same capabilities as MKB-300.	$2,195
● Kurzweil	MIDI Board	88 key velocity-sensitive, touch calibration, 8 MIDI outs, 12 control devices assignable to any MIDI parameter, include foot pedals, sliders, wheels, buttons...	$2,200

MIDI Expander Modules

(Modules which are directly related to an earlier keyboard unit are listed under MIDI Synthesizers.)

● Roland	MKS-7 Super Quartet	2-voice polyphonic Melody section, 4 voice chord section, Monophonic Bass, and Rhythm section, 220 preset sounds for Melody, Chords, and Bass, 11 digital PCM sounds for Rhythm Sounds are modifiable. This and a computer will go a long way.	$1,095
	EM-101 Sound Plus	8-voice polyphonic module, 16 presets, attack and velocity sensitive.	$295
	MKS-20 Digital Piano Sound Module	16-voice module offering 8 digital sound sources using Structured Adaptive Synthesis—a Roland digital sampling synthesis for digital emulation of keyboards. Parametric eq, chorus, MIDI in and through.	$1,695
	MKS-80 Super Jupiter	Velocity and pressure sensitive, Jupiter-type sounds. 8-voice, 64 memories, cartridge for 64 more, step programmable through the little window.	$2,495
	MPG-80	Super Jupiter programmer. Faster & easier. Knobs & Sliders Forever.	$495
	MKS-30 Planet S	6-Voice, 64 memories, cartridge for 64 more. Dynamics-responsive, stereo chorus. Works with PG-200 programmer.	$995
	MKS-10 Planet P	16-voice polyphonic piano sound module. Eight instrument sounds, four effects with rate and depth controls.	$1,095
	DDR-30	Digital drum module.	$1,395
● 360 Systems	MIDI Bass	Sampled basses in a box. Touch sensitive, follows pitch bends. Large chip library of all the standard basses, electric, acoustic, and synthesized.	
		2 sounds:	$399
		4 sounds:	$499
		Alternate chips:	$50
		360 Systems, 18730 Oxnard Street, Tarzana, CA 91354. (818) 342-3127.	
● Korg	MR-16	MIDI controllable 16 output rhythm sound unit.	
● Oberheim	Xpander	12 VCO's, 6-voice, each can be sent to a different MIDI channel, mind-boggling routing possibilities. The most flexible analog?	$2,995

MIDI Pianos and Organs

● Kawai	EP308M	88 key electric grand piano with MIDI. A sixty-year-old Japanese piano company, they should know how to do it right. Hammer still hits string, vibration is converted to electrical signal, sorry, therefore no MIDI in. But wait! There's a MIDI out, so it might be o.k. after all.	$5,695
	EP705M	75 key electric upright piano with MIDI out. Velocity sensitive, eight memory control patches. (Same setup as EP308M).	$2,495
	KX series 1000 2000 5000	Nice, big, fat, home organs for fun and hernias. Drawbars, auto chords, rhythm patterns. Independent MIDI channel assignments to upper keyboard, lower keyboard, and pedals. Yahoo!	

		Kawai America Corp., 24200 South Vermont Ave., Harbor City, CA 90170.	
● Yamaha	CP70M	A famous and functional instrument MIDIfied. You'll still have to tune it, but hey...76 keys, 7 band graphic EQ, MIDI out.	$4,695
	CP80M	88 keys, hammers, & strings on this baby. Make the roadies move it. 7 band graphic, MIDI out.	$5,695
	CP60M	An upright, still electric/acoustic. Still heavy. So what. 7 band graphic, MIDI out. These three pianos also sport two effects loops apiece and a variable stereo tremelo setup.	$2,695
● Korg	MPK-130	13-pedal MIDI pedalboard—(1 octave, 2 C's) omni or polymode. Korg, 89 Frost St., Westbury, N.Y. 11590. (516) 333-9100.	$495
● WERSI	Alpha DX350S	Big home organ with digital features, 16 addressable MIDI channels. Build the kit! They have even bigger ones!	

Kit: **$4,300**
Assembled: **$7,900**

WERSI, 1720 Hempstead Rd., P.O. Box 5318 Lancaster PA 17601 (217) 299-4327.

MIDI Samplers

● Ensoniq	Mirage	8-voice pitch bend and modulation sent and received on MIDI. Velocity sensitive.	$1695
		Input sampling filter increases sampling rate to 50kHz.	$149.95
	Mirage Digital Multi-Sampler	Rack-mount version samples in increments, preserving character of acoustic instruments. Can handle two samples at once in a playing situation. Upper and lower banks, or two voices on one key.	$1,395
● Akai	S612	Rack-mount (no keyboard), uses disk drive storage, 32K bandwidth, 6-voice.	$895
● Decillionix	DX-1	Software-based sound sampling system for Apple IIe or II +. Cheap!! (If you have the computer.) Flexible editing capabilities. Monophonic.	$349
	MIDI-Madness	The link to any MIDI controller. Velocity sensing, 5 octave tuning. Decillionix, P.O. Box 70985, Sunnyvale CA 94086. (408) 732-7758	$99
● Sequential	Prophet 2000	5 octaves, velocity sensitive, weighted action, multiple assigning, user-sampling, sample editing, disk-drive, synthesis as well as sampling.	$2599
● Korg	SDD-2000	Sampling digital delay, monophonic 1 second at 18 kHz MIDI triggerable.	$695
	SG-1	12 voices, 76 keys, uses four pre-sampled piano sounds with ROM card updates	$1695
	DSS-1	12-bit sampler, 8-voice, disk drive, with full sampling features.	$2500
● PPG Wave	Waveterm	Eight samples assignable to keyboard, 24 tracks of digital events. Much more.	$11,000
	Waveterm B	Upgrade for the PPG Wave 2.3 computer. 16-bit encoding, variable polyphony, extensive editing capability.	$2,850
● E-mu	Emulator II	8-voice, crossfading between sounds, arpeggiator, sound splicing, different sample on each key if desired. Neat digital editing with analog controls.	$7,995
● Europa Technologies	Swiss MDB Window Recorder	Monophonic, but 18-bit resolution.	

3 Seconds **$2,995**
6 Seconds **$3,395**
12 Seconds **$4,650**
24 Seconds **$5,995**

● Fairlight	CMI	Does anything. MIDI interface & software $500 extra. Sucker. Fairlight Instruments, 2945 Westwood Blvd., Los Angeles, CA 90064. (213) 470-6280	$32,000 base
● Synclavier		Does everything else. MIDI's built-in though. 1 in, 4 out. Expandable to 8 in, 32 out. New England Digital, (802) 295-5800	$50,000 base

● Kurzweil	250	88 keys, 12 voices, sequencer, famous piano sounds, keyboard splitting (into six) MIDI in, out, thru, assignable levers, sliders, switches. I want one.	$10,715
	250 Expander	It's the 250 without the keyboard. Has all the factory presets, plus 12-track sequencer.	$9,980
	Sound Modeling Program	Necessary for sampling your own sounds on the 250. 5-25kHz, 20 seconds at full band widths. Many other editing and processing features. New version has 5 to 50 kHz response, a considerable improvement. Price is the same, upgrade for old model is $250 installation charge.	$1,995
	Sound Block A	Sound module with 15 new voices, 84 keyboards setups.	
	Mac Attach	Offline storage of sound files, setups and sequences.	$195

MIDI Drum Machines

● Roland	TR909	Ancestor of TR707. Harder to program, but tunable. Two MIDI outs, sync signal, cassette data storage.	$1,195
	TR707	15 digitally-recorded drums, 10 individual outs, triggerable, accepts velocity information. Usable as a MIDI source also. RAM cartridge auto memory.	$595
	TR727	A 707 with Latin Percussion sounds.	$595
	TR505	16 drum sounds, somewhat less memory than 707. Can run on batteries.	
● E-mu	Drumulator	12 digitally-recorded sounds, replaceable with alternate chips. Triggerable with velocity information.	$745
	SP-12	Pre-programmed, digitally sampled sounds as well as user-sampling capability. Tuning, delay, volume, tempo changes programmable. Touch sensitive play buttons, full triggering and MIDI, battery back-up memory.	$2,745
● Yamaha	RX11	29 digitally-recorded sounds, auto-correct and free-time. Individual panning, stereo out as well as 12-channel individual outs. RAM storage.	$895
	RX15	12 keys, 15 sounds. Stereo out, MIDI in/out.	$495
	RX21	How cheap can a digital drum machine get? Does great stuff for the dough.	$275
● Sequential Circuits	Drumtracks	13 digitally recorded sounds, 6 channels out, tuning controls, can memorize different tunings within a song, as well as a global volume change.	$1,295
	TOM	8 digital sounds, tuning, stereo pan for each, human factor control.	$795
● Linn	Linn 9000	18 digitally-recorded drums, velocity and pressure-sensitive pads, free and auto-correct time, vast sound library.	$4,990
		32-track sequencer on board. Disk drive option at...	$950
		Sampling system option is...	$690
	LinnDrum Midistudio	16-pad digital drum machine with disk-drive, user sampling, and 32-track MIDI recorder in a portable 2-piece package. Available early 1986. Linn is out of business at press time.	$5990
● J.L. Cooper	Sound Chest II	Triggerable with MIDI, drum pads, or tape sources, voice modules include tuning, decay rate, dynamic filter, dynamic tuning. For J.L. Cooper see MIDI Hardware.	$2,995
● Dynacord	Percuter-S	8-channel digital drums with replaceable plug-in modules. Triggerable with full-size drum pad kit, cute little triggering mics, or else there's....	
	Big Brain	16-channel sequencer, will run 2 Percuter-S units. Dynamics controls, 50 song memory.	
	Boomer	Digital sampler. 128 and 256-K plug-in sample modules, which can then be triggered from the unit or installed in a Percuter-S. (Contact Europa Technology, see Lync controller).	
● Casio	RZ-1	12 drum sources, individual outs, MIDI velocity sensitive. 100 pattern memories, 20 songs. On-board sampling capability, 4 samples storable. All data storable via cassette dump.	$599
● WERSI	CX5	The catalog was in German, but it looks as though they've been doing their homework. 64 factory presets, 32 custom presets, 32 cartridge presets, rhythm computer on board. For address, see WERSI, MIDI Organs.	

● Simmons	SDS9	The famous Simmons electronic drum kit, sports MIDI outs to trigger from the set and ins to trigger the set from elswhere.	$2,195
	SDS EPB	A digital sampler. Stores sampled sounds in EPROM chips. Not directly MIDIfied, but since the chips are used in the SDS9, they are accessible to a MIDI system.	$795
● Roland	Pad-8 Octapad	MIDI pad controller. 8 pads, independently assignable to any MIDI instrument. 3 parameters programmable, Curve, Minimum Velocity, Gate Time.	$550
	DDR-30	Rack-mount digital drumkit. Six voices, 32 sounds available, MIDI triggerable, sound modification. Many sound parameters, memory cartridge.	$1,895
	PD-10	Bass drum pad.	$225
	PD-20	Snare drum/tom pads.	$115
● Oberheim	DX	Second generation DMX, now MIDI compatible. DMX vied with LinnDrum for supremacy. Compatible with existing DX sound kit library. Oberheim Electronics, 2250 S. Barrington Ave., Los Angeles, CA 90064. (213) 473-6574.	$1,395

MIDI Guitars

● Roland	GR 700	64 presets, this synthesizer speaks for the Roland guitars. 64 sound memories, big foot controller, MIDI out. Individual string asignments, dynamics, chorus. M-16 memory cartridge available.	$1995
	PG200	Analog programmer for GR-700.	$295
	GR707	The guitar with the stabilizer bar, 2 humbuckers, whammy bar, the Roland hexagonal pickup.	$1150
	G-505	Strat type, no stabilizer, hexagonal bridge pickup, whammy bar, 3 single-coil pickups.	$925
	G-202	Ash body, 2 humbuckers, hexagonal pickup.	$1,295
	G-808	1-piece neck, exotic woods, 2 humbuckers, hexagonal pickup.	$1,295
	G-303	Maple and mahogany, 2 humbuckers, hexagonal pickup.	$930
	GR 77B	4-voice bass synth. MIDI out, 64 sound memories, memory cartridge, big pedal board, PG800 programmer for easy sound modifications. Cartridge compatible with JX-8P.	$1,995
	G-77	Bass guitar controller. Has that stabilizer box.	$1,150
	G-88	Thru-body, 1 piece neck bass, hexagonal pickup.	$1,195
	G-33	Maple neck, ash body orthodox setup, hexagonal pickup. Also available are guitars from *Steinberger, Gibson, Hamer* and *Pedulla* with Roland guts.	$895
● Ibanez		Advanced string bend capabilities, each preset can control 2 synths simultaneously or independently. Key transpose, independently assignable string selects. And it's a guitar! Looks and plays like a nice one.	$1,200
● Octave Plateau		Voyetra MIDI guitar, separate output for natural guitar sounds, onboard keypad, onboard readout. Microprocessor scans strings and frets for activity, converts info to MIDI signals. Two-hand neck playing possible. Due out 1986.	$1,995
● Synthaxe		Due out in 1986. It'll do a lot. Expensive. Synthaxe Ltd. Four Seasons House, 102b Woodstock Road, Witney, Oxfordshire. 0993-76910.	

Pitch-to-MIDI Converters

| ● Fairlight | Voicetracker | 10-octave range around middle C. It does it. Sing through your synth. Play sax through it. Fart through it. The future is here. Anything converts to MIDI. Oh yes—it'll draw a picture of it, too. Fairlight Instruments, 2945 Westwood Blvd., Los Angeles CA 90064. (213) 470-6280. | $2,495 |

● Cherry Lane	Pitchrider 4000	8-bit microprocessor as opposed to 32-bit in the Fairlight. Less individual tailoring features, but it's cheap! Velocity and pressure sensitive also. Cherry Lane, 110 Midland Ave., Box 430, Port Chester, N.Y. 10753 (914) 937-8601	$495
	Pitchrider 7000	Polyphonic version for guitar players. Cherry Lane makes it, Kramer is the licensed distributor. For info contact your Kramer dealer.	$1000
● Gentle Electric	Model 101 Pitch and Envelope Follower	MIDI retrofit for this analog device coming out in 1986. MIDI unit promised as well.	$400 $1,000

Gentle Electric, P.O. Box 132, Delta CO 81416. (303) 874-8054.

MIDI Sequencers

● Roland	MC-500	Real time, step time, stores on floppy disk. 5 tracks, track merging, editing, tempo changes programmable.	$1,095
	MSQ 100	One-track, can reassign MIDI channels from the same instrument (select send/receive channel).	$625
	MSQ 700	8-track polyphonic, records and plays back any MIDI info. You can merge tracks. Play into it in free time and auto correct or not. Step programs as well, of course.	$1,195
● Yamaha	QX1	Real-time and step-programmable. 8-track, 32 song memory on floppy disk, edits MIDI control functions, can bounce tracks. The mother of the TX 816 tone generator system.	$1,195
	QX7	2-track sequencer, real time memory and auto-correct. Track-merging, cassette interface.	$2,795
	CX5M Music Computer	An 8-voice sequencer as well as on-screen DX7 programmer, not to mention FM synthesizer. Great computer to start.	$469
● Korg	SQD-1	16 MIDI channel, MIDI recorder, playback, disk drive. 15,000 note capacity real-time or step programmable, punch-in and punch-out, copy, insert, delete modes.	$695
● Casio	SZ-1	4-track, 1,800 note capacity, real time/step time, RAM external memory or cassette dump, runs on batteries or AC.	$399
● Linn	Linn Sequencer	32-track, 16-channel digital MIDI recorder. Available with remote featuring tape recorder-type controls. Available without disk drive for	$1,995 $1,295
● Akai	ME-20A	Arpeggiates chords input from a MIDI instrument. Three arpeggio patterns. Can also be used as a polyphonic sequencer up to 1056 notes.	$149.95
● Indus Systems	MIDI DJ	Stand alone 5¼-inch floppy disk recorder/sequencer, 2 track, 16 MIDI channels for track. 12,000 note memory. Indus Systems, 9304 Deering Ave., Chatsworth CA 91311. (818) 882-9600.	$595

MIDI Digital Delays and Reverbs

● Yamaha	REV7	Stereo programmable digital reverb. 30 presets, 60 effects programs. MIDI program selection from keyboards and other MIDI devices.	$1,195
	D-1500	Digital delay, 16 MIDI memory locations.	$895
● Peavey	4000	Programmable effects processor, up to 4 seconds delay, 15 kHz bandwidth in delays up to 1 second, 10 patches available. 7-pole anti-aliasing filter minimizes signal coloration.	$895
● Roland	SRV 2000	Programmable digital reverb. 32 memories accessible through MIDI devices.	$1495
	SDE 2500	Programmable digital delay, 64 memories, accessible with MIDI program change info.	$795
● Lexicon	PCM 70	Parameter control through dynamic MIDI, unique feature. Programmable digital effects processor. Great specs. 40 plus factory programs, 50 user programs.	$2,295

		Lexicon Inc., 60 Turner Street, Waltham MA 02154. (617) 891-6790.	
● Dynacord	PDD 14	Programmable digital delay, 16 programs, 15 kHz frequency range, MIDI switchable.	
	DRP 16 (M)	Stereo digital reverb, 8 programs. The Dynacord footswitch runs it too.	
	Bank B	Extra 8 program memory for PDD14 and DRP16(M). Europa Technologies. (See Lync Controller)	
● Akai	ME10D	Digitally delays MIDI signal to 1000 M/sec. max. Also raises or lowers octave. Neat.	$149.95
● ART	DR1	Stereo in and out, 16-bit digital reverb. 14 kHz band width, 100 user presets, 30 factory, updatable, remote control. Applied Research & Technology Inc., 215 Tremont St., Rochester, NY 14608. (716) 436-2720	$1,295
● Ibanez	DUE 4000	Digital delay, chorus/flanger, distortion, compressor, 128 programs, MIDI accessible.	
	EPP 400	Five effects loops, MIDI controllable.	
● Korg	SDD 2000	MIDI equipped 64-program sampling digital delay 1 second at 18 kHz, 4 seconds max.	$695

MIDI Amplifiers

● Peavey	Programax 10	210 watts, 2 12-inch speakers, ten patch settings programmable with external MIDI controller. Saturation, tones, reverb effects.	$995
	RMC TBA 2000	Remote MIDI controller for feet. Selects any of ten program presets, dual MIDI channel control capability, auxiliary bypass function.	
● Dynacord	Reference Series	Big tube amps, with MIDI brains. Reverb level controls, graphic equalizer, chorus, and external effects can be programmed in 16 separate patches. 11-button footswitch. Good idea. Europa Technology. (See Lync Controller)	

MIDI Hardware

● Roland	MPU-401	Intelligent MIDI interface for Apple and Commodore computers	$200
	MPU-101	This is it—the ultimate. It turns MIDI data back into *analog* signals. Omigod. Synchronize lighting equipment, run CV synthesizers, short out the neighborhood.	$295
	LPK-1	Mod kits for GR Synthesizer. Guitar and bass retrofits.	$260
	STK-1	Authorized service centers only.	
	MPU 103	Reassigns MIDI data from one channel to another. Simple.	$260
	MPU 104	More and better switching. 104 has 5 MIDI-in and 1 MIDI through.	$90
	and 105	105 has 1 MIDI in and 5 through. Together you've got yourself a patchbay.	$110
	MD-8	Connects MIDI synths with DCB synths (Jupiter 8).	$295
	MM-4	MIDI thru box. 1 in, 4 out.	$70
	OP-8M	Interface between CV and MIDI or DCB devices.	$895
	MKS-900	Signal indicator, displays any channel's key-on info with 88 LED's. Can also be used as channel filter. 1 in, 5 out.	
● Forte	MIDI-mod	Custom-installed MIDI retrofit for acoustic grands, Yamaha, Kawai electric grands. Detects on/off, velocity, damper pedal. Prices include installation. Forte Music, Box, 6322, San Jose, CA 95150.	$475 to $1,495
● Ibanez	MIU8	MIDI interface. 1 in, 8 out, remote controller for your foot.	
● TOA	D-4	4-input stereo rack mixer expandable to 10 in. Features MIDI-thru patching. TOA Electronics Inc., 480 Carlton Court, South San Francisco, CA 94080. (415) 588-2538.	$500
● Assimilation	MIDI Conductor	Interface for Macintosh computers, 2 in, 2 out.	$89
● Akai	ME-15F	MIDI mixer for volume levels. 8 in, 2 out.	$149.95
● Yamaha	YMC10	Converts MIDI signal into FSK tape sync signal. Record that on one	$120

		track of your multitrack recorder, and you're synched up for later. 2 MIDI outs.	
● JL Cooper Electronics	MIDI Disk	Disk Drive, 3½-inch micro floppy format for loading or offloading MIDI data from any MIDI device.	$895
	MIDI Switch Box 16/20	16 in, 20 out, programmable	$1395
	Effects Switcher	16 x 16 matrix for effects switching. 64 MIDI memory locations.	$2,000
		MIDI interface for Apple IIC from Roland MPU-401. J.L. Cooper Electronics, 1931 Pontius Ave., West Los Angeles, CA 90041. (213) 473-8771. J.L. Cooper makes many more MIDI products. Call for info.	$139
● Yamaha	YME8	MIDI through box, 2 in, 8 thru/out.	$90
● Garfield Electronics	MINI DOC	MIDI timing coordinator for disparate MIDI units. Syncopation even possible by offsetting two clock circuits.	$595
	Doctor Click 2	Updated Doctor Click. High-class synchronizer.	$1195
	Master Beat	Simultaneous production of all sync formats. Six fixed clocks. Third generation sync technology.	$2,495
	Multi Trigger	Six channel drum triggering.	$395
	Drum Doctor	Six channel universal drum triggering unit, assignable MIDI outs.	$1495
	Nano Doc	Drum machine synchronizer, allows instruments to sync to tape.	$250
	MIDI Adapter	Sync MIDI to any clock output	$200
	FSK Adapter	FSK to MIDI codes	$200
		Garfield Electronics, P.O. Box 1941, Burbank, CA 91507. (818) 840-8939.	
● Korg	Compu-Dump	ROM retrofit for DW 8000, EX-8000 and Korg Poly 800. You pay installation charge.	Free!
	KMT-60	MIDI through box, 1 in, 6 out.	$69.95
	KMS-30	Interface for MIDI to non-MIDI drum machines, sequencers and tape recorders, especially small Korg digital drums.	$195
	MEX-8000	Remote unit programmer for all Korg synths, using system exclusive data. 256 patches.	$195
	DYP-1	Vocoder/harmonizer, all digital signal processing.	$1195
● Decillionix	MIDI-Madness	Link between any MIDI keyboard and Decillionix DX-1 sound sampling, on Apple II computers, velocity sensing, sound tuning. Decillionix, Box 70985, Sunnyvale, CA 94086.	$99
● Opcode Systems	MIDIMAC	Interface for Macintosh. Opcode Systems, 1040 Ramona, Palo Alto, CA., 94301 (415) 321-8977	$125
● Syntech		Midi interfaces with tape sync for Apple IIe, II plus, Commodore, and IBM PC.	$130 to $300
	S-14	MIDI thru boxes 1 in/4 thru	$69.95
	S-28	2 in/8 thru	$149.95
	S-81	8 in/1 out	$149.95
		For Syntech see Software.	
● Wersi		MIDI interface for Commodore 64	$95
		Synchronizer	$85
● Hybrid Arts	MidiMate	Interface box for Atari computers. For Hybrid Arts see Software.	$199.50
● Octave Plateau	OP4001	Intelligent MIDI interface for IBM. For Octave Plateau see Synthesizers.	$295
● MusicData		Interface for MusicData programs, Commodore 64, Apple II plus and IIe. For MusicData see Software.	$100
● Passport	MIDI interface	Apple drum sync	$150
		tape sync	$300
		Commodore drum sync	$130
		tape sync	$200
	MIDI Pro interface	Apple IIc, IBM and Macintosh. For Passport see Software.	$299.95
● Moog	Song Producer	MIDI in, thru, 4 outs. See description under software	$395
● Simmons	MTM	8 channel programmable interface, translates audio signals into MIDI code and MIDI signals into triggers. Makes SDS7 MIDI compatible, among other things.	$1195
● Lemi		An Italian company which makes a variety of MIDI devices, including a wireless MIDI system. Lemi, 37 Corso Matteotti, Turin, Italy.	
● Kamlet Electronics	MIDI Patcher	4-in, 8-out MIDI switch box	$269.00

MIDI Control Systems

● Ibanez	MIU8 interface unit	1 MIDI input, 8 MIDI out on any 16 channels. Hoshino USA Inc., P.O. Box 886, Bensalem, PA 19020. (215) 639-8670.	
	IFC60 Intelligent Foot controller	Recall 128 MIDI programs, control 8 MIDI devices, large L.E.D. display, 15 foot cable. Chesbro Music Co., 327 Broadway, Idaho Falls, 83401. (208) 522-8691	
	EPP400	A MIDI controllable electronic patchbay. Provides 5 effects, loops (three in stereo), 128 programmable preset locations controlling on/off and loop sequence.	
● Dynacord	MCCI Control Computer	Rack-mount, 4 MIDI outs, over any 16 channels, 99 programs of any combination. Dynacord's ubiquitous footswitch unit runs this as well as most of their other products. Contact Europa Technology (see Lync Keyboard Controller).	$995
● Roland	SBX-80	Reads and generates MIDI, SMPTE, Sync-24, and Time Base signals. For video and audio sync functions.	$1,195
● Voyce	LX-4	Four channel MIDI controller. Change patch number, volume, and octave settings of 4 synthesizers. Also splits any master keyboard into three zones, remembers 99 4-way patches. Internal battery backup. Voyce Music, P.O. Box 27862, San Diego, CA 92128. (619) 549-0581.	$495

Synchronizable Tape Systems

● Synchronous Technologies	SMPL System	Allows Commodore computer to talk to a SMPTE-reading tape deck through RS-232 port. Does punch-ins, locates.	$1,000
	Chase-Lock	Does many SMPTE-based synchronizing functions.	$2,000
● Fostex	4050	Autolocator, syncs MIDI to SMPTE.	$1,250
	A-8 (modified)	8-track on ¼-inch tape, has RS-232 port.	
	B-16	16-track on ½-inch, has RS-232 port.	
● Tascam	42, 48, 52, 58	These decks can all sync using the RS-232 port.	
	MS-16		
● Otari	MS-70	16-track, 1-inch. Also SMPTE-controllable through RS-232 port.	

MIDI Software

● Octave Plateau	Sequencer Plus	For IBM PC. Requires Roland MPU-401 or OP-4001. MIDI interface.	$495
	Rev. 2	Update for Rev. 1.	$75
	Patch Master	Patch Librarian for IBM PC and compatibles.	
● Roland	MPS	Eight-track, IBM PC Compositor and arranging tool. Transcribes, edits and prints out super music notation. Recording and playback are interactive with the score mode, so you can really fix it in the mix. Requires MP 401 and MIF-IBM card.	$500
	MUSE	Eight-track sequencer/editor for Apple IIplus and C-64. Straightforward but powerful. Uses MPU-401 and MIF-APL card, or MPU-C64. Free-time and time correction.	$150
● Moog	Song Producer MIDI Command, Songstepper, Sync Command	User-friendly, inexpensive, and good manual. Real time/step mode hardware/software MIDI drum/sync, color video computer system. Interfaces with Commodore. Moog Electronics, 2500 Walden Ave., Buffalo, NY 14225.	$395
● Personal Composer		Records, edits, stores voices, notates, by Jim Miller. Includes computer, printer, program disk, MPU-401 interface. Standard Productions, 1314 34th Ave., San Francisco, CA 94122. (415) 681-9854.	$3,000

MusicWorks	MacMIDI	MegaTrack—16 channel recorder for Apple.	$150
		MIDI Works music printing.	$100
		Sync. or SMPTE interfaces.	$250/300
		DX/TX Voicepatch Librarian	$150
		MusicWorks, 18 Haviland, Boston MA 02115. (617) 266-2886.	
● Dr. T's Music Software for Commodore Computers		Keyboard controlled sequencer.	$125
		Echo-Plus.	$90
		CZ Patch Librarian.	$65
		DX7 Patch Librarian.	$75
		Dr. T's Music Software, 66 Louise Road, Chestnut Hill, MA 02617. (617) 926-3564.	
● OpCode Systems	MIDI Mac	Sequencer.	$150
		Patch Librarian. DX7, TX7, Roland, CZ, Oberheim, Fender Polaris	$50
		Patch Editor.	$99
		OpCode Systems, 1040 Ramona, Palo Alto, CA 94301. (415) 321-8977.	
● Sight & Sound	MIDI Ensemble	255 tracks. Gulp. For IBM PC.	
		Sight & Sound, P.O. Box 27, New Berlin, WI 53151. (414) 784-5105	$495
● Hybrid Arts	Miditrack II	For Atari (400,600,800,800XL, 1200)	$349
	Miditrack III	For Atari 130XE (W128K).	$374
	Miditrack C	Commodore C64 or SX-64.	$349
	Miditrack PC	For IBM.	$449
	Miditrack Modem	Software for Atari	$39
	Midipatch	Software for DX or CZ.	$79
		Hybrid Arts Inc., 11920 W. Olympic Blvd., Los Angeles, CA 90064. (213) 826-3777.	
● Micro Music	MIDI software	Memory dump for Casio CZ-101 and CZ 1000.	
		Micro Music, Fruchtalle 19, D-2000, Hamburg 20, West Germany.	
● Mimetics	DX-Connect	DX and TX editing on-screen.	$149
		Mimetics Corp., P.O. Box 60238 Sta. A, Palo Alto, CA 94306. (408) 741-0117.	
● Nexus		FM Drawing Board—Apple II or IIe.	$200
		Nexus Computer Consultants Inc., 212 Main St., Toronto, Ontario, Canada M4E 2W1. (416) 690-0983.	
● Korg	KSQ-800	4-track sequencer program for Commodore and Apple IIe/+ computers.	$99.50
	MS-11	8-track version.	$149.95
● Ensoniq		Mirage Visual Editing System for Apple II and IIe.	$299
		Ensoniq Corp., 263 Great Valley Parkway, Malvern, PA 19355. (215) 647-3930.	
● Syntech Music	Digital Studio	8-track MIDI studio, Commodore or Apple. IBM coming soon.	$225.95
● Roland	Super Jupiter Editor	For IBM PC-works with MPU-401 and MKS80.	
● Passport	Polywriter	Music printing software.	
	Lead sheeter	Cheaper music printing software for Apple II and IIe.	$99
	MIDI Player	Sequencing set organizer for live work	$99.95
	MIDI/4 Plus	MIDI recording software, 4-track.	$99.95
	The Music Shop	Music printing software for Commodore 64 or 128	$149.95
	MIDI 8	Apple IIe, II+ or Commodore 64	$149.95
	Master Tracks	16 channel sequencer for Apple and Commodore, step-time editor, real-time editor, song editor. Patch librarians available for all major synthesizers.	$249.95
		Passport Designs, 625 Miramontes St., Half Moon Bay, CA 94019. (415) 726-6280.	
● Syntech		Keyboard Patch controller software using Commodore 64.	$225.95
		Syntech Corp. 23958 Craftsman Rd., Calabasas, CA 91302. (818) 704-8509.	
● Syntech	Studio I-II-III	8-track for Apple IIe, Commodore 64, or IBM. Reads and writes sync.	$225.95
	Songplayer	28-song live performance setup. For Commodore 64.	$129.95
		Keyboard patch controller software using Commodore 64	$225.95
		Syntech Corp., 23958 Craftsman Rd., Calabasas, CA., 91302. (818) 704-8509	
● Southworth Music Systems	Total Music	Full-featured sequencing, editing, and transcribing for MacIntosh 512K.	$489
	Total Music 250	Customized Total Music program developed with Kurzweil for the K250.	$550

		Upgrade of original Total Music Southworth Music Systems, 91 Ann Lee Road, Harvard, MA, 01451 (617) 772-9471	**$75**
● **Cherry Lane**	**Connections** **Texture** **DX-Heaven** **CZ-Rider**	8-track recording for Apple. Pattern/Part recording, Apple and IBM. On-screen DX voice editing, librarian for Apple. On-screen CZ-101 editing, librarian for Apple. Cherry Lane, 110 Midland Ave., Box 430, Port Chester, N.Y. 10573 (914) 937-8601.	**$149** **$149** **$149** **$149**
● **Wersi**	**MIDI-16 Track** **Music Editor**	16-track for Commodore 64 Music printing. For Wersi see Midi Organs and Pianos	**$195** **$225**
● **MusicData**	**MIDI Sequencer** **MIDI** **Synchronizer**	16-track for Commodore 64, Apple IIplus/IIe External clock, sync-to-tape, Commodore 64, Apple IIplus/IIe Music Data has plenty of other programs for C-64 and Apple, including filers, librarians, and delays; they also make plenty of cassette-loaded patches for MIDI synths and drumboxes. MusicData Inc., 8444 Wilshire Blvd., Beverly Hills, CA 90211 (213) 655-3580	**$150** **$100**
● **Great Wave**	**Concert Ware**	8-track studio for 512K Macintosh, interface not included. Great Wave Software, Box 5847, Stanford, CA. 94305, (415) 325-2202	**$139.95**
● **Korg**	**Voice Editor**	For Commodore 64 and Apple IIe. Includes Librarian, Program/Parameter, and Sequence Recorder/Editor for Poly 800, DW-8000, EX-8000	**$99.95**
● **Digidesign**	**Sound Designer**	Emulator II waveform displays on Macintosh for high-powered sample editing. Digital synthesis also possible on Mac. Digidesign, Inc., 920 Commercial, Palo Alto, CA. 94303 (415) 494-8811	
● **Blank** **Software**	**Sound Lab**	Advanced Ensoniq sound design for Apple, Macintosh. Endorsed by Ensoniq. Blank Software, 2442 Clay Street, San Francisco, CA. 94115 (415) 922-8538	**$399**
● **Decillionix**		Sound sampling and MIDI products for Apple IIe. See Samplers.	